Running the Gauntlet

Other Books by Bernard Edwards

Masters Next to God
They Sank the Red Dragon
The Fighting Tramps
The Grey Widow-Maker
Blood and Bushido
SOS – Men Against the Sea
Salvo!
*Attack and Sink**
*Dönitz and the Wolf Packs**
Return of the Coffin Ships
*Beware Raiders!**
*The Road to Russia**
*The Quiet Heroes**
*The Twilight of the U-boats**
Beware the Grey Widow-Maker
*Death in the Doldrums**
*Japan's Blitzkrieg**
*War of the U-boats**
*Royal Navy Versus the Slave Trade**
*The Cruel Sea Retold**
*War Under the Red Ensign 1914–1918**
*The Wolf Packs Gather**
*Convoy Will Scatter**
*The Decoys**
*U-boats Beyond Biscay**
*Churchill's Thin Grey Line**
*From Hunter to Hunted**

* Denotes titles in print with Pen & Sword Books

Running the Gauntlet

Cargo Liners Under Fire
1939–1945

Bernard Edwards

Pen & Sword

MARITIME

First published in Great Britain in 2022 by
Pen & Sword Maritime
An imprint of
Pen & Sword Books Ltd
Yorkshire – Philadelphia

ISBN 978 1 39909 786 4

Printed and bound in the UK by CPI Group (UK) Ltd, Croydon, CR0 4YY.

Pen & Sword Books Limited incorporates the imprints of Atlas, Archaeology,
Aviation, Discovery, Family History, Fiction, History, Maritime, Military,
Military Classics, Politics, Select, Transport, True Crime, Air World, Frontline
Publishing, Leo Cooper, Remember When, Seaforth Publishing, The Praetorian
Press, Wharncliffe Local History, Wharncliffe Transport, Wharncliffe True
Crime and White Owl.

For a complete list of Pen & Sword titles please contact

PEN & SWORD BOOKS LIMITED
47 Church Street, Barnsley, South Yorkshire, S70 2AS, England
E-mail: enquiries@pen-and-sword.co.uk
Website: www.pen-and-sword.co.uk

Or
PEN AND SWORD BOOKS
1950 Lawrence Rd, Havertown, PA 19083, USA
E-mail: Uspen-and-sword@casematepublishers.com
Website: www.penandswordbooks.com

Contents

They threw everything at us. The planes came over in droves of a hundred, and submarines tried to get us too. There were a few poor souls going to heaven that day . . . Nobody slept. You did your watch then went straight to getting ammunition for the gunners from the lockers. People ask if you were scared. You went past that stage. You went on automatic.

Able Seaman Bob Sanders, aged 16
Brisbane Star, Operation PEDESTAL

Preface

When war came again to Europe in September 1939, Great Britain owned and operated a fleet of some 4,000 merchant ships, almost two thirds of the world's commercial shipping. All trades, from coastal waters to the deep oceans, were served, and it was a rare day when the Red Ensign was not in evidence in port or at sea. Prominent among these ships were the fast cargo carriers of the liner companies, who offered a regular, advertised service between specified ports. Blue Funnel, Clan Line and City Line dominated the East and Far East trades, while Blue Star, Port Line and the New Zealand Shipping Company covered the meat trades with South America, Australia and New Zealand.

Between the wars, the cargo liners were considered to be the crème de la crème of British merchant shipping, the mainstays of the Empire, carrying manufactured goods outwards and returning loaded to the gunwales with the spoils of colonialism. Air travel was not yet within reach of the masses, and most of these ships had good, but basic accommodation for twelve passengers, which was principally occupied by minor government officials and trading companies' employees travelling to and from home leave. They were fast ships, generally making in excess of 12 knots, in an age when the average merchantman was often hard pressed to maintain steerage way. They were sturdily built, well maintained, and officered by 'Company's men', i.e. career-minded sailors who offered the shipowner their expertise and loyalty in exchange for continuity of employment on a regular run. They wore their uniform with pride and adhered to the rules with good grace. Little wonder that, when war came, the cargo liners were very much in demand.

In the opening days of the conflict these ships sailed alone, relying on their superior speed to outwit the enemy. Then, as the demands of war grew, more and more they found themselves at the beck and call of the Admiralty. Selected for special missions, they became the risk takers, running the gauntlet of enemy shot and shell as required. The risks they took were fearsome, and their losses in ships and men were grievous, yet they were rarely found wanting.

Author's note

To add to the authenticity of this book I have relied heavily on eye-witness accounts. There can be no better storyteller than one who was there, and I offer my belated thanks to those who had the foresight to put pen to paper. Future generations will read and wonder.

CHAPTER ONE

The Gentleman Raider

The rattle of crockery from the Officers' Pantry below warned the *Norseman*'s wireless operator that lunch was on the way and it was almost time to go off watch. He reached for his pen and began to write up the log.

There was little to report. It was Sunday, 30 September 1939, and the Cable & Wireless ship was on station off the north-east coast of Brazil, a lonely spot where even the cry of the seagull was subdued. Furthermore, the war was only four weeks old, and any other ships in the area were keeping strict radio silence. Radio watchkeeping in these troubled times had been reduced to sheer boredom. No longer was the *Norseman*'s operator able to while away the watch chatting to passing ships or distant shore stations; he was condemned to re-reading the same old well-thumbed paperback, with one ear tuned to nothing but the irritating crackle of atmospherics. It seemed to him that although radio silence might be necessary in the Western Appproaches, where Hitler's U-boats were busy laying waste to Allied shipping, out here, 3,000 miles removed from the conflict, such a precaution was hardly called for. He glanced out of the window. Overhead, the sky was an untroubled blue, a gentle breeze was hard pressed to raise even a ripple on an even bluer sea, and only the occasional wisp of smoke marred a horizon that was as sharp as a whetted knife. The cold, wet Western Approaches were truly a world away.

The operator was about to throw the off switch on his receiver when a faint burst of morse broke the silence of the ether. He snatched up his headphones and listened. When it came again, the message was still faint, but unmistakable in its meaning: *RRR RRR 09 08S 3404W CLEMENT GUNNED*. The prefix RRR was code for 'I am being attacked by an enemy surface raider'. Somewhere, 2,500 miles south of the *Norseman*, a British ship was in trouble.

The cable ship's operator passed the distress message to the *Norseman*'s Captain, who despite the danger of giving away his own ship's position to the enemy, decided to break radio silence to warn the Admiralty of the presence of a German surface raider off Brazil.

All efforts to contact shore stations in the West Indies were in vain, and in desperation the *Norseman*'s operator went over to short wave and called Portishead Radio, some 3,000 miles away in the Bristol Channel. Here, he also drew a blank, for although Portishead was an extremely powerful station, normally able to keep in touch with ships worldwide, the atmospheric conditions were adverse.

Fortunately, later in the day the *Norseman* did suceed in contacting the American steamer *Mormacrio*, then in the vicinity of Pernambuco. She repeated the *Clement*'s RRR signal to a nearby shore station, which in turn passed it to the British Consul in Pernambuco. By this devious route the signal finally reached the Admiralty in London.

The 5,051-ton *Clement*, owned by the Booth Steamship Company of Liverpool, was one of a 30-strong fleet of medium-sized cargo/passenger carriers whose stock-in-trade had for many years been an advertised service from Liverpool to North Brazil via Oporto, Lisbon and Madeira. On this occasion, having left Liverpool some weeks earlier, the *Clement* was engaged on an intermediate run from New York to Bahia carrying 20,000 cases of kerosene. Packed two 5-gallon drums to a case, this amounted to a total of 200,000 gallons of potential fire hazard, a cargo Captain Harris and those who sailed with him would be heartily glad to see the back of. The *Clement* then being only 200 miles north of Bahia, journey's end was almost in sight.

Captain Frederick Charles Pearce Harris, RNR, immaculate as ever in crisp white tropical uniform, had enjoyed a full English breakfast, and was ready for the day's work. Being Sunday, it was Captain's inspection of the accommodation and galleys at eleven o'clock, but first he must write a letter to Head Office advising them of the progress of the voyage so far, which he was happy to report had been without incident.

Contributing to Captain Harris's good spirits was the knowledge that having put 4,000 miles of the Atlantic behind her, the *Clement* was well out of the war now raging in Europe. Although hostilities were yet to break out on land, in the Western Approaches there were reports of mayhem. Ships were sinking, men were dying. Meanwhile, the *Clement* continued to sail unchallenged and was unlikely to come within shooting range of the enemy. There were rumours that a German commerce raider was somewhere in the area, but the threat was so vague as to be ignored.

Harris put down his pen when the whistle of the bridge voicepipe shrilled urgently. It was Third Officer Gill, who had the watch on the bridge, reporting an unidentified warship sighted on the port bow, and bearing down on the *Clement* at speed.

Hurrying to the bridge, Captain Harris examined the approaching ship through his binoculars. She was end-on, and difficult to identify, but she certainly had the distinctive silhouette of a man-of-war – and a large one at that. Her high bow-wave indicated she was closing at something like 30 knots. Under normal circumstances, this would have been alarming. But no alarm bells rang for Captain Harris. Prior to sailing from New York he had been informed that the British light cruiser *Ajax* was in the area, and at some time the *Clement* was quite likely to be challenged and boarded. He ordered the ensign to be hoisted and warned the engine room to stand by for orders.

That the *Clement* was about to be challenged was true enough, but not by HMS *Ajax* or any other British ship. Her challenger was the German pocket battleship *Admiral Graf Spee*, whose namesake's origins lay deep in the history of Anglo-German relations. The link went back a quarter of a century to November 1914, when the German East Asia Squadron, under *Vizeadmiral* Maximilian Johannes Maria Hubert Graf von Spee, inflicted a humiliating defeat on the Royal Navy at the Battle of Coronel.

The German East Asia Squadron was made up of the two heavy cruisers *Scharnhorst* and *Gneisenau*, the light cruisers *Dresden*, *Leipzig* and *Nürnberg*, and a number of supply colliers. On 1 November 1914, this force met up with with a British squadron at Coronel, off the coast of Chile. The British squadron consisted of the armoured cruisers *Good Hope* and *Monmouth*, the light cruiser *Glasgow*, and the armed merchant cruiser *Otranto*, all under the command of Rear Admiral Christopher Cradock.

Gun for gun, the two opposing forces were evenly matched, but there the similarity ended. Whilst the German ships were all comparatively new, *Good Hope* and *Monmouth* were built at the turn of the century and *Glasgow* was five years old and in need of modernization. Furthermore, the men manning these British ships were largely reservists, sadly lacking in gunnery training. The armed merchant cruiser *Otranto*, on the other hand, was an 18-knot ex-passenger liner mounting a handful of ancient 4.7s firing over open sights, and likely to prove more of a liability than an asset in a fight. This Cradock was quick to realize and he detached *Otranto* out of harm's way before the action began.

The battle was joined as the sun was going down on 1 November, with von Spee craftily positioning his ships in the shadow of the coast. The British ships were silhouetted by the light of the setting sun, and hopelessly outclassed from the start. The combined gunfire of *Scharnhorst* and *Gneisenau* quickly over-whelmed *Good Hope* and *Monmouth*, and both the British heavy cruisers were sunk with all hands, some 1,600 men being lost. HMS *Glasgow* was forced to run and escaped only by virtue of her superior speed.

The Battle of Coronel was the Royal Navy's first significant defeat since the days of Nelson and Napoleon, and it caused consternation at home and abroad. Anticipating a swift response from the vastly superior British forces he knew to be in the area, *Vizeadmiral* Graf von Spee lost no time in quitting the Pacific. He is quoted as saying, 'You must not forget that I am home-less. I cannot reach Germany. . . I must fight my way through the seas of the world doing as much mischief as I can, until my ammunition is exhausted, or a foe far superior in power suc-ceeds in catching me. But it will cost the wretches dearly before they take me down.'

As von Spee had anticipated, the Royal Navy was quick to seek retribution for the loss of the *Good Hope* and *Monmouth*, and the victorious East Asia Squadron now became the hunted. The German ships fled east, rounding Cape Horn undetected. They might well have got clean away, had von Spee not been tempted to strike one last blow against his enemies. Moving into the South Atlantic, the squadron closed the Falkland Islands intent on bombarding the Royal Navy's coaling station at Port Stanley. Von Spee had assumed the base would be unguarded, but unfortunately for him, the pre-dreadnought battleship HMS *Canopus*, mounting four 12-inch guns, had been beached just inside the breakwaters. As the German ships approached, *Canopus* opened fire with her big guns, some of her shells fall-ing uncomfortably close to *Scharnhorst* and *Gneisenau*. Caught unawares, and fearful that his heavy cruisers might receive serious damage, von Spee abandoned the attack and made off at full speed.

And that would have been that, had not HMS *Inflexible* and HMS *Invincible* been patrolling waters nearby. Alerted by *Canopus*, the two 20,000-ton battlecruisers set off in pursuit of the enemy squadron.

The British ships had a top speed of 26½ knots, and the chase was short-lived. In just over an hour, the German vessels were being pounded by the guns of *Inflexible* and *Invincible*, each of which mounted four twin 12-inch turrets. *Scharnhorst* and *Gneisenau* replied but their 8-inch guns were no match for the combined firepower of the British battlecruisers. Of the East Asia Squadron, only the light cruiser *Dresden* survived. *Scharnhorst*, *Gneisenau*, *Leipzig* and *Nürnberg* all went to the bottom, taking with them some 2,200 men, including their leader *Vizeadmiral* Maximilian Graf von Spee and his two sons Ferdinand and Heinrich, who were serving as lieutenants in the squadron.

Although the East Asia Squadron was roundly defeated at the Falklands, Maximilian von Spee was hailed as a hero in Germany. When the dust of 1918 had settled and the German Navy was again becoming a force to be reckoned with, his name would be remembered and honoured.

On the outbreak of war in July 1914, Germany was ranked as one of the world's great naval powers. Her Imperial Navy then consisted of 14 dreadnought battleships, 22 pre-dreadnoughts, 4 battlecruisers, 9 armoured cruisers, 41 cruisers, 144 destroyers, 28 submarines, and various small craft. The Treaty of Versailles, signed in June 1919, had been designed to put an end to Germany's warlike ambitions, and one of the restrictions imposed on her was the reduction of her fleet to 6 pre-dreadnought battleships, each of not more than 10,000 tons displacement, 6 light cruisers, 12 destroyers, and 12 torpedo boats. In the light of the damage they had done to Allied merchant shipping during the war, no submarines were to be allowed.

As might be expected, these savage cuts were not well received in Germany, and when Adolf Hitler came to power in 1933 a veil of secrecy was drawn around German naval shipbuilding activity. Little control was exercised by the Treaty Powers, leaving the design engineers of Hitler's new *Reichsmarine* free to work their magic. One of the end results was the building of three battlecruisers of the *Deutschland* class, one of which was named *Admiral Graf Spee* in memory of the hero of Coronel.

The *Graf Spee*, classified as a pocket battleship by the Admiralty, was ready for sea in January 1936. In order to conform with the restrictions of the Treaty of Versailles, she was declared as having a load displacement of 10,000 tons, whereas she actually displaced 16,280 tons fully loaded. Powered by eight MAN 9-cylinder diesels geared to two propellers, she had a top speed of 28½ knots, and a cruising range of 16,300 miles at 18½ knots. Her armament consisted of six 11-inch guns in two triple turrets, eight 5.9-inch in single turrets and three 3.5-inch. Eight 21-inch torpedo tubes completed this very impressive array of weaponry. She also carried two catapult-launched Arado Ar 196 floatplanes and, for the first time in any German warship, was equipped with the new 50cm *Seetakt* radar. The *panzerschiffe Admiral Graf Spee* was a far cry from the modest home-defence cruiser envisaged by the Treaty of Versailles.

After three months working up in the Baltic and North Sea, the *Graf Spee* joined the German fleet, and over the following two years was involved in the Spanish Civil War carrying out non-intervention patrols for the Nationalists. In February 1938, with *Kapitän zur See* Hans Langsdorff in command, she embarked on a world tour to show the flag, which included an appearance at Spithead for the Coronation Review of King George VI in May 1937.

Born within the sound of the sea on Rügen Island in 1894, Hans Wilhelm Langsdorff was predestined to serve in Germany's navy. When he was four years old, the Langsdorffs moved to Dusseldorf, taking a house near the estate of Count Rudolf von Spee, whose son Maximilian would later become the hero of Coronel and the Falklands. Young Langsdorff fell under the spell of this naval family and was enrolled at the Naval Academy in Kiel on leaving school. By the time the First World War broke out, he had attained the rank of *Leutnant zur See*, and subsequently saw action at Jutland. After the war, he took up a series of shore-based appointments.

When Hitler became *Reichschancellor*, Langsdorff requested a return to sea, but it was not until late 1936, with the rank of *Kapitänleutnant*, that he was appointed to the newly-commissioned *panzerschiffe Admiral Graf Spee* on the staff of Admiral Boehm.

His career then took off and in January 1937 Langsdorff was promoted to *Kapitän zur See*. In October 1938, he was given command of the *Graf Spee*. Less than a year later, on 21 August 1939, he sailed out of Wilhelmshaven, bound for the South Atlantic.

Before crossing the Equator, the *Graf Spee* made a rendezvous with her supply ship *Altmark* in a remote spot south of the Canary Islands. The 11,000-ton *Altmark* was one of five tankers built to supply German surface raiders. Commissioned in Kiel in 1939 under the command of *Kapitän* Heinrich Dau, she was a twin-screw motor vessel powered by four 9-cylinder MAN diesels which gave her a top speed of 21 knots and a range of 12,500 miles at 15 knots. She was manned by naval personnel and equipped with three 5.9-inch and two 1.5-inch guns, plus four 20mm AA cannon and eight machine-guns, a formidable array of weaponry for a supposedly non-combatant ship. In her tanks, the *Altmark* carried some 13,000 tons of diesel oil, while her cargo hold was packed with ammunition, spare parts and food – everything required to keep the *Graf Spee* at sea without the need to seek out a friendly port.

The two ships met up on 1 September. The weather was fine, the sea calm, and as he had not yet received orders to commence hostilities, *Kapitän* Langsdorff saw no reason to hurry the transfer of supplies. The operation stretched out for another ten days, during which war was declared, but was brought to an abrupt end when the *Graf Spee*'s Arado, keeping watch aloft, signalled that it had sighted an unidentified warship approaching.

Anxious to avoid a confrontation, Langsdorff broke off the supply operation and both German ships steamed away at high speed. This proved to be a wise move, the approaching ship being the British heavy cruiser HMS *Cumberland*. Attached to the South American Division of the 2nd Cruiser Squadron, the *Cumberland* was a 31½ knot ship armed with eight 8-inch guns, a force to be reckoned with. She would have almost certainly sunk the *Altmark* on sight, and presented a real challenge to the *Graf Spee* herself.

Fifteen days later, nearing the coast of Brazil, Langsdorff at last received the news he had been waiting for. A signal from Berlin authorized him to begin his campaign against Allied merchant shipping in the area. He moved in closer to the coast and for many long and tedious hours combed the shipping lanes for potential victims. At last, on 30 September, when the *Graf Spee* was some 60 miles east of Pernambuco, a wisp of smoke appeared on the horizon.

The *Clement* had sailed from Pernambuco at first light that morning, and was some eighteen hours steaming from Bahia, where she would be rid of the last of her hazardous cargo. Journey's end was in sight, and an air of satisfied relaxation had settled over the British ship. Then, at about 1130 hrs, the war reared its ugly head. Third Officer Gill, who had the watch on the bridge, wrote in his report to the Admiralty:

> I sighted a battleship 4 points on the port bow on the horizon. From the time I sighted it, it was making a bee-line for us all the way. Three or four minutes later, a plane appeared – more on the port quarter. She circled around the CLEMENT and flashed a message to the battleship giving the information he wanted – whether we were armed or not, I suppose.

Called to the bridge, Captain Harris was not overly concerned, being under the impression that the fast approaching warship was the British light cruiser HMS *Ajax*, which he knew to be in the area. He recorded the events that followed:

> I could see no flags, only that it was a man-o'-war. It was about four or five miles off with a huge bow-wave as if he was coming in at 30 knots. A few minutes later, I heard a buzzing sound and a seaplane passed. I was not worried as I knew the AJAX had one. We exposed the name board. The plane went round the bow and over the port side, then aft, and came over the ship again, and started firing. Meanwhile, the warship, her guns trained on the CLEMENT menacingly, was drawing near.

Having embarked on her voyage while the euphoria of Neville Chamberlain's 'Peace in our time' still prevailed, the *Clement* was completely unarmed and unprepared for war, and Captain Harris wisely stopped his engines and ordered the lifeboats to be swung out ready for lowering. Some five minutes later, when much of the way was off the ship, he ordered his crew to abandon her. While this operation was in progress, Harris instructed Radio Officer Rainford to send out the RRR signal, indicating that the ship was being attacked by a surface raider. The distress message was promptly answered by a Brazilian merchant ship. Harris then supervised the burning of all the ship's code books and secret papers in the galley fire.

When all four lifeboats were fully loaded and lowered to the water, Captain Harris took a quick turn around the decks to ensure that no one had been left behind. He then boarded his own boat, and they pushed off. They had just cleared the ship's side, when a powerful launch manned by men in German naval uniform came sweeping around the stern of the *Clement*.

The launch drew alongside Harris's boat and an officer called for the Captain and Chief Engineer to declare themselves. As both Harris and Chief Engineer Bryant were in uniform with badges of rank plain for all to see, they had no option but to comply. They were taken on board the German launch, which then went alongside the *Clement*. Captain Harris wrote in his report:

> There were about 10 men and 2 officers there. I climbed up the boat ladder. They were putting a heaving line down, and hauling up a sack of bombs; there were about 12 tins of these in the sack. Then they told me to stay where I was and asked for the Chief Engineer. Five or ten minutes later, they came back again with two sacks of loot, but no bombs. The Chief Engineer was with them when they came back in the picket boat.

Chief Engineer Bryant later explained:

> When I was on board the CLEMENT with the boarding party, one man with a revolver in his hand took charge and said 'Come down to the engine room', and when we were there he told me to open the sea valve. I immediately opened the tank main injection, he did not seem to know much about it. These valves would merely fill the ballast tanks and would not flood the ship. We then came up. Whilst I was with this officer the other men were going round the ship putting bags of bombs around the vessel.

Captain Harris's report continues:

> Having left the side of the CLEMENT they then said

'Put your lifejackets on; the ship may blow up any minute.' We got away from the CLEMENT and headed for
the man-o'-war. We went under her stern and, as we were
approaching her stern, I saw very distinctly ADMIRAL
SCHEER on the starboard quarter in raised letters painted
over. The whole ship was painted grey. There was no doubt
in my mind that these were her original name marks.

Third Officer Gill also identified the enemy warship as
the *Admiral Scheer*, but both he and Captain Harris were mistaken, as it is on record that the *Admiral Scheer* was at anchor off
Wilhelmshaven at the time.

Captain Harris's report goes on:

They hooked the picket boat on and lifted her up level
with the rail and told the Chief and me to step out on
deck. The Boarding Officer went and reported to the
Captain. We followed up the staircase to the bridge. When
there, we met the Captain and ten officers. He saluted me
and said 'I am sorry, Captain, but I will have to sink your
ship. It is war.' Shortly afterwards, he said 'I believe you
have destroyed your confidential papers?' I said 'Yes'.
He answered 'I expected it. That is the usual thing.' Then
the ADMIRAL SCHEER steamed round on to the other
side of the CLEMENT – on to the lee side – the starboard
side – so that we were head to stern – starboard side of
the ADMIRAL SCHEER to the starboard side of the
CLEMENT, about 1000 yards off.

Langsdorff then studied the abandoned merchantman through
his binoculars, and after a few minutes, turned to Harris, and
with a genuine note of regret in his voice, informed him that
he was going to sink his ship with a torpedo. The *Graf Spee* was
then manoeuvred so that her stern-mounted torpedo tubes were
aimed at the Clement, and a single torpedo was fired. Although
the range was less than 1,000 yards, the torpedo missed, passing
about 50 feet ahead of the British ship.

Not surprisingly, Langsdorff was visibly annoyed at this dis-
play of poor marksmanship, and even more upset when a second
torpedo missed the target, passing no more than 25 feet astern of
the *Clement*. Concealing his humiliation in front of his prisoners,

he said, 'Now we will use the guns', hoping no doubt to give the impression that all was to plan.

The *Graf Spee* now steamed around the Clement's stern, came up on her port quarter, and then turned stern-on again. The two ships were, in Captain Harris's estimation about 2,500 yards apart. He later wrote:

> They started with the 6" gun and fired about 25 rounds. They were not happy about that either – some were going short and some were hitting. Some of the officers could speak English well, and one said 'If we were further away we would hit but we are too close.' They gave us cotton wool during the firing to put in our ears.
>
> Then they said 'Now we are going to use the big guns.' They fired about five rounds of the 11" from the forward turret. . . The five shots pierced the CLEMENT in the bow and set her on fire – I could see red flames. Gradually, she settled down by the bow and they did not fire any more. She went down gradually by the head until she was dead upright.

This demonstration of the *Graf Spee*'s poor shooting did not augur well for her future career as a commerce raider. Both ships were lying stopped at close range, the weather was fine, the sea calm, and the *Clement,* having very little cargo left on board, was flying high out of the water. And yet, it took two torpedoes, twenty-five rounds of 6-inch, and five rounds of 11-inch to sink her. The only excuse that came to be given for this poor showing was that it was the first time the cruiser had fired in anger and, for that matter, the first time in over twenty years that an enemy merchantman had been sunk by a German surface raider. Obviously, there were lessons to be learned.

When the *Clement* finally gave up the struggle and slipped below the waves, the *Graf Spee* made off at full speed in a south-easterly direction, Langsdorff no doubt anxious to quit the scene before a British warship arrived in answer to Harris's RRR signal. The two prisoners were allowed to stay on the bridge for another hour, when Langsdorff sent for them and asked them to give their word that they would not attempt any sabotage or espionage, in return for which they would be allowed full run of the ship. Harris and Bryant agreed without hesitation. They then shook hands with Langsdorff, after which they were accorded what can only be described as VIP treatment. Captain Harris records:

> The Commander (not the Captain of the ship) then said 'Come with me' and took us to his own cabin. He gave us cigars and iced beer. Then he wrote out in English this order from the Captain about sabotage and let us read it and asked us to sign it. We did so. After about an hour an orderly came and said that our cabin was ready. The Commander took us there himself. It had evidently been an officers' cabin. Two officers were turned out so that we could use it. On the after bulkhead I noticed a lifebuoy photo frame painted in white with 'Reichschiff Admiral Scheer' on it. Then a steward came and asked us if we would have something to eat, and brought a huge dish of cold meat, tongue and sausage, bread and butter, a pot of tea, and a small bottle of rum to put in the tea. People kept coming in and out, asking if we were quite happy, and talked to us conversationally.
>
> After the meal, an officer came along with tooth brushes, a nail brush, soap and towels, and said 'You may be here a week or a fortnight. Would you like a razor, or will you go to the barber's shop? There are three barbers here.' Just to give them confidence, I said I would go to the barber's shop; they said 'That will be better than giving you a razor.' Then an officer said 'Come with me' and took us to the hospital, which looked to me like an action station. The ratings we saw sitting there had gas masks with tins, which they were handling, trying on etc. Two officers were set to watch the Chief Engineer and myself. We sat there for half an hour. Then the telephone rang and they said 'We are stopping another ship. We shall probably be able to put you on board.' Then another officer came down and the two watching us were released and we were taken up on deck. A picket boat was ready over the side in the slings. One of the officers said 'The Captain wants to speak to you' and the Captain, leaning over the bridge, said 'Goodbye, Captain. Good luck.'

Harris and Bryant had been captive aboard the *Graf Spee* for some five hours, during which time the *Clement*'s four lifeboats, containing forty-seven survivors, were hove-to close by, their occupants witnesses to the slow and agonizing end of their ship.

Dusk was closing in when the *Clement,* reduced to a smoking hulk, finally slipped beneath the waves, and the *Graf Spee* made off hurriedly into the encroaching darkness. For a long while, the thud of her powerful engines could still be heard, but that too faded into the night. It was now deathly quiet, with only the slap of the waves and the creak of the boat timbers to disturb the silence. It was then that the survivors began to feel alone and helpless.

A weak cheer was raised when, about half an hour later, the lights of a ship were seen to the north. Sails were hoisted and course set to close the ship, but with the coming of darkness the wind had risen, creating a rough sea, which was on the beam as the boats tried to claw their way to the northward. Progress was pitifully slow, and the lights of the ship were rapidly disappearing into the night. Distress flares were lit, but they produced no response. Hope of an early rescue had gone. It was then decided to head west for the coast of Brazil.

During the course of the night, the boats became separated, and by dawn next day, Sunday 1 October, they were out of sight of each other. But this was a busy shipping lane, and at about 0800 hrs Third Officer Gill's boat, containing sixteen men, was sighted by the Brazilian steamer *Itatinga,* which picked them up and landed them at Maceio, some 60 miles from Pernambuco. The other three lifeboats, carrying a total of thirty-one survivors, made a landfall near Maceio later that day.

Captain Harris and Chief Engineer Bryant, who had been put aboard the 3,478-ton Greek steamer *Papalemos* by Captain Langsdorff, had a rather more prolonged voyage. The *Papalemos* was on passage from Brazil to Freetown, and nine days elapsed before the two officers were landed at St. Vincent, in the Cape Verde Islands. They languished there for seventeen days, before being taken to Le Havre by a Dutch merchantman, where they were put ashore, wiser but none the worse for their experience. They had been the guests of a true gentleman of the old *Reichsmarine.* Those who came after them would find the war a very different proposition.

CHAPTER TWO

The Miracle of Dunkirk

Despite the ominous rumblings from the far side of the Channel, all seemed well in England's green and pleasant land on that fine Sunday morning in early September 1939. Then, as the sound of church bells rang out across the fields to mingle with the whirr of combine harvesters, Prime Minister Neville Chamberlain broadcast a solemn message to the nation:

> I am speaking to you from the Cabinet Room at 10 Downing Street. This morning the British Ambassador in Berlin handed the German Government a final note, stating that unless we heard from them by 11 o'clock that they were prepared at once to withdraw their troops from Poland a state of war would exist between us. I have to tell you now that no such undertaking has been received and that consequently this country is at war with Germany.

The eternal optimists, whose glasses were always half-full, said it would all be over by Christmas and, for the second time in twenty-five years, the British Expeditionary Force girded its loins and set out across the Channel to 'assist our French allies in putting the Boche back in their place again.' The whole thing had an all too familiar ring.

Nine months later, on 10 May 1940, after a protracted 'phoney war' in which the protagonists thumbed their noses at each other across an undisturbed No Man's Land, Hitler's panzers fired up their tanks, bypassed the 'impregnable' Maginot Line, and surged into the Low Countries. British and French forces moved to meet them, but from the start it was obvious that they were hopelessly outclassed.

The German armies, under the command of General Fedor von Bock and General Gerd von Rundstedt, consisted of some 60,000 men, 771 tanks and 141 pieces of heavy artillery, supported by an air umbrella of 1,470 fighters and bombers of the

Luftwaffe. On the ground, they were outnumbered by the British and French forces opposing them, but while the Allies were largely equipped with First World War weapons, the Germans had the finest and most modern that Alfred Krupp's factories could produce. Belgian and Dutch resistance crumbled before the might of the Panzers, and by the middle of May, the British and French armies, thoroughly demoralized, found themselves fighting a 'strategic withdrawal' towards the Channel coast. It was a retreat that quickly became a scramble for survival, with abandoned vehicles blocking the roads and a flood of refugees heading in the opposite direction. In later years, Winston Churchill, who by then had become Prime Minister, wrote:

> The whole root and core and brain of the British Army seemed about to perish upon the field or to be led into an ignominious and starving captivity, and if the war against the 3rd Reich was to be won there would have to be an army left to win it.

With no other alternative available, Operation DYNAMO was set in train, its object being to bring the remnants of the BEF back across the Channel. The chosen evacuation point was the French port of Dunkirk, at the northern end of the Dover Strait, and close to the Belgian border.

Enclosed by two long stone breakwaters, and with a broad, shelving beach, Dunkirk harbour contained a port with modern facilities, including electric cranes, and was only 39 miles by sea from Dover. As the retreating Allied armies fell back on the port, it was planned to send in the Royal Navy's destroyers and transports to evacuate the troops and the bulk of their weaponry. However, what should have been a relatively orderly operation descended into a rout when 300 bombers, protected by 550 fighters of the Luftwaffe made a series of devastating raids on Dunkirk and its port, dropping 15,000 high-explosive and 30,000 incendiary bombs. The town was set ablaze, 1,000 of its inhabitants were killed and the docks completely flattened. Operation DYNAMO became a race against time to pluck the survivors of the BEF from the gently shelving beaches of Dunkirk. It was estimated that, at the very best, some 25,000 men might be rescued before they were overwhelmed by Hitler's Panzers. All tanks, artillery and vehicles would be left behind.

To carry out the proposed evacuation, the Royal Navy sent in the anti-aircraft cruiser HMS *Calcutta,* eight destroyers, and a number of corvettes and trawlers. They were joined by a fleet of small merchantmen, cross-Channel ferries, paddle steamers and tugs, all requisitioned by the Admiralty. Unfortunately, owing to the shelving nature of Dunkirk's beaches, none of these craft was able to get close enough inshore to take off the bulk of the men who were by then sheltering from the wrath of the Luftwaffe in the sand dunes, in their thousands.

Now the call went out for the 'little ships', and the Admiralty scoured the south coast of England and the Thames Estuary for suitable small craft to act as shuttles between the beaches and the big ships lying off shore in Dunkirk harbour. Private yachts, Thames barges, inshore fishing boats, lifeboats, speedboats, any small craft capable of surviving the 39-mile crossing from Dover, were taken up for service. Buoys were laid to mark the many shoals and dangerous wrecks that fouled the waters of the Dover Strait, copies of charts were hastily printed and distributed, and a 300-strong armada of 'little ships' set out for Dunkirk. Most of the craft requisitioned were manned by Royal Navy crews, but a significant number of civilians were also involved.

Meanwhile, Dunkirk had deteriorated into chaos. Under attack from the air by Ju 88s and Stukas of the Luftwaffe, and shelled by German artillery, Allied troops had sheltered in the dunes, waiting their turn to be taken off by the Royal Navy. On the first day of Operation DYNAMO only 7,669 Allied soldiers had been rescued, and on the basis of that most of the BEF seemed likely to end up in captivity. Unable to go closer in because of the shallow water, the destroyers resorted to berthing alongside the harbour breakwaters, an extremely risky operation. It went well until the Luftwaffe realized what was being attempted, then the bombers came swooping in. One British destroyer was sunk and a French destroyer damaged as she tried to join in the rescue. Two other British destroyers were hit but were able to clear the harbour, each with 500 men on board. The Isle of Man Steam Packet Company's ferry *Fenella* tried to emulate the destroyers but was hit by three bombs and sank alongside the East Mole. The majority of the 650 men she had taken on board escaped, and were picked up by the paddle steamer *Crested Eagle,* but she too was then bombed and sunk. The evacuation via the breakwaters was not abandoned, but it was slow work, and the queues on the beaches were growing longer by the hour.

The first of the small craft arrived on the 28th and they immediately began ferrying troops from the beaches out to the waiting ships in deep water. Again, this worked well until the Germans became aware of what was happening. The Luftwaffe was called in and the defenceless little boats came under heavy attack from the air. Magnificent under fire, they persisted in their effort to save the stranded troops, but the slaughter was grievous. Another solution was needed.

It so happened that the answer to their dilemma was at that time lying in Southampton – twelve newly built Assault Landing Craft (ACLs), with their crews already in training. Flat bottomed, armed with AA cannon, protected by armour plating, and drawing only 2 feet when loaded, the ACLs were designed to carry fifty men and their equipment. It only needed a suitable ship to take them across to Dunkirk. That ship was then in London docks discharging a cargo she had brought in from India.

The 6,787-ton *Clan Macalister* was a British cargo liner owned by Clan Line Steamers of Glasgow. Built on the Clyde in 1930, she was powered by a single screw, triple-expansion steam engine which gave her a top speed of 13 knots. She was no 'ocean flyer', but with heavy lift derricks fore and aft, she was well equipped to handle the ACLs.

Clan Line Steamers Ltd, also known as Cayzer, Irvine & Co., was among the best of British merchant shipping companies. Its ships were built to the highest specifications at the company's own shipyard on the Clyde, they were immaculately maintained, and manned by British officers and Indian ratings, all 'Company's men'. Clan Line's ships had served the Admiralty well as supply ships and auxiliaries during the 1914–18 war, coping with any task, no matter how difficult and dangerous. This, added to the fact that Clan Line officers wore very similar gold braid to that of the Royal Navy, had earned the company the honorary title of the 'Scots Navy'.

The *Clan Macalister* was already known to the Admiralty, having been requisitioned earlier in 1940 to carry the guns and vehicles of the 115th Field Regiment, Royal Artillery, across the Channel to reinforce the BEF. Her cargo discharge was speeded up, and she was rushed to Southampton to pick up the waiting

ALCs and their crews. Her master, Captain R. W. Mackie, was briefed to take her into Dunkirk.

The distance from the Solent to Dunkirk is only 160 miles, but the route lies through one of the busiest and most hazard-strewn waters in the world, the Straits of Dover. In l940, although the traffic through the straits was greatly reduced, the proliferation of shoals, sandbanks and wrecks was still there, and as eager as ever to snare the careless navigator. In summer and winter alike there was the possibility of dense fog forming without warning, Now, added to the natural dangers were the minefields, British and German, some charted, some not.

Captain Mackie was a well experienced navigator, and certainly no stranger to the Straits of Dover, which he had traversed many times pre-war. However, this passage promised to be very different and he was more than a little apprehensive as, with the 9-ton ALCs lashed down on her hatch-tops, he took the *Clan Macalister* out of the Solent in the late afternoon of 28 May 1940. Hugging the English coast as far as Dungeness, Mackie eased past the Varne Shoal and Goodwin Sands, crossed over to the French side and began his approach to Dunkirk at the Dyck light vessel. It was a well trodden path, in peacetime plagued by hordes of fishermen and day-tripper yachts, now virtually deserted except for the occasional British or French naval patrol boat.

The *Clan Macalister* reached the Dyck light vessel, where in normal times she would have picked up her pilot for Dunkirk, just as dusk was setting in. The battle for survival being fought in the port was already evident, the whole area being covered by a curtain of thick black smoke, through which could be seen the ominous flash of gunfire and exploding bombs.

The approach to Dunkirk harbour is littered by a maze of dangerous shoals, around which Mackie was now expected to wend his way without the help of a local pilot. It was a daunting prospect. He later wrote in his report:

> I was to proceed at once as near to Dunkirk as possible, there to discharge the ALCs and their crews, and then it was suggested that I might make a rendezvous with Commander Cassidi where the boats, if damaged, could come and be repaired. These were verbal orders. I was given a route through the Downs to Dunkirk also the

position of some dangerous wrecks. I did not like proceeding in the dark through the Downs among those wrecks
and so many ships at anchor without lights, and I told
Commander Cassidi that I should have a pilot. The naval
officer had departed by this time. I laid down on the chart
all the route and wrecks and I told Commander Cassidi
again I did not like the job in the dark. He then said, 'If
you don't like to go, Captain, give me a course to steer
and put the boats in the water and I'll take them across.'
I felt that was a challenge to our ability, so I started to
heave up right away, and was under way by 1 a.m. on
the 29th. I picked our way through the Downs, narrowly missing one of the wrecks to the westward of the
Goodwin Sands. At about 3.30 a.m. we heard an SOS –
'Unknown steamer torpedoed at Kaempfe Buoy' – and,
as our route was to pass south of that buoy, I wanted to
avoid the area and asked permission from a patrol vessel to steer direct for Dunkirk across a 'Forbidden to
Anchor' area, but he said 'No'. I spoke to Commander
Cassidi and he said, 'You can take me as close as you can,
Captain, discharge my craft and then go back home.'

The above exchange serves to illustrate the wide gulf that
often exists between the Royal and Merchant Navies when con-
fronted by a dangerous situation. On the one hand, Captain
Mackie saw his primary duty as the safety of his ship and the
delivery of his cargo intact, which called for a cautious approach.
Commander Cassidi, on the other hand, was trained to adopt a
more aggressive approach, even if that meant risking the ship
and the lives of those on board. In the end, Mackie's authority prevailed and he weaved his way slowly and carefully
through the hidden dangers to find a safe anchorage inside
the breakwaters of Dunkirk harbour.

While the *Clan Macalister* was making her cautious approach
to Dunkirk, the toll of lost ships and men was rising. Just before
midnight, the destroyer HMS *Wakeful* had sailed for Dover, having on board 650 troops she had snatched from the beaches. She
had just cleared the approaches to the port and was altering
course to the westward, when lookouts on board sighted the
tracks of two torpedoes racing towards the ship. A swift alteration

of course avoided one torpedo, but the other struck the destroyer amidships, breaking her back. The two halves of the ship settled on the bottom in the shallow water, but most of the troops were asleep below decks, and were drowned.

Fortunately, there were a number of ships in the immediate area, so the response to *Wakeful*'s SOS was immediate. First on the scene were the drifters *Comfort* and *Nautilus*, returning to Dunkirk from Dover. They were followed by the minesweeper *Gossamer*, bound for Dover with 420 troops, then the destroyer *Grafton* with 800 and the drifter *Lydd* with 300, also on their way back across the Channel.

Boats were lowered, and survivors from the torpedoed *Wakeful* were being picked up, when the *Grafton* was also torpedoed. In the melee that followed, *Grafton*, though by then sinking, opened fire on the *Comfort*, believing her to be an enemy E-boat. *Lydd* added to the disaster by ramming and sinking *Comfort*. Only one of the drifter's crew and four of those she had picked up from the *Wakeful* were saved.

No one knows how many men died out there in the darkness of the Channel that night. It was believed that the torpedoes had come from *U-69*, but that was never confirmed. And there was worse to follow. Later that day, two destroyers engaged in the evacuation, HMS *Mackay* and HMS *Montrose* collided and both ran aground, while the Isle of Man Steam Packet Company's paddle steamer *Fenella* hit a magnetic mine and blew up. To add to all that, German dive bombers were constantly attacking the ships as they went about their errands of mercy. Such was the chaos of the Dunkirk beaches that day.

Captain Mackie's report continues:

> We started to discharge the craft and had just lifted our first into the air when the destroyer Vanquisher dashed past at full speed and set up such a wash as to cause the ship to roll so heavily that the men lost control of the guys and the craft swung violently from side to side with the crew on board. The Second Officer then lowered the craft down a little to try to get control of it but it damaged itself and the other one on deck so they became unfit for service.

Thanks to the unsolicited help of the Royal Navy, the *Clan Macalister* had wrecked the first two ALCs, but as soon as the ship steadied up the discharge continued. At the best of times putting the 9-ton craft in the water would not have been an easy operation; with German shells and bombs dropping all around her and the stench of acrid smoke in the air, it took iron discipline and steady nerves to carry on. Fortunately, the men who manned the *Clan Macalister* had a surfeit of both. The remaining craft were landed without further mishap and Commander Cassidi and his two lieutenants took them in to the beaches.

His mission completed, Captain Mackie signalled the nearest British destroyer and asked for further orders. The reply came back, 'Carry out your original orders.' As Mackie had no orders beyond the delivery of the ALCs to Dunkirk, he decided to join in the frenzied evacuation and take on board as many of the fleeing soldiers as possible before turning back across the Channel. He signalled his intentions to the destroyer, whose commander obviously had no idea of how to use his services, and was told to move his anchorage further to the east, and await orders.

Sensing that his ship was being regarded as something of a nuisance by the Navy, Mackie took matters into his own hands. He moved in as close to the beach as his draught would allow and began taking men on board from the small boats plying to and from the sand dunes. Some of Cassidi's landing craft also took the opportunity of bringing men out. The *Clan Macalister* being the largest ship in the harbour by far, it was not long before the German bombers turned their attention to her. Captain Mackie's report tells what happened next:

> About 3.45 p.m. an air raid was made over the ship and when it had passed we found our vessel on fire aft in No.5 hold, on deck and on the gun platform. No.5 hatch beams had been cut and twisted. The coamings burst out and the hatches all dropped below and were on fire. On the port side there was a large hole in the deck, the plates being pushed downwards at the after end of the hatch abreast of the tonnage opening, also another large hole in the wooden sheathed deck further aft, and the crews' quarters were a mess of twisted beams and wreckage. On the starboard side about the same distance aft, there was another hole where a bomb had penetrated the deck and burst, as the hatch coamings on

that side were full of holes and most of the dead were lying on that side as far as I could see. When we were seen to be on fire HMS *Malcolm* came alongside and started taking the soldiers off and some of the crew that were injured. Two lines of hose were passed on board and started playing into No.5 hold, but could not reach the gun platform, which was alight. The ship's hose was brought into use, but as the deck service pipe had been broken and holed in places, we did not get much pressure. While this was going on a party were dumping petrol out of the two damaged ALCs also ammunition from around the gun platform (the high-angle gun breech block was seen to be wrenched off). While the wounded and the troops were being transferred to HMS *Malcolm* some of the native crew had got on board and the commander intended to put them back on the ship, but the aeroplanes were coming at us again, so she cast off, her commander giving us a new course to steer. We continued with the hose aft, but the fire soon gained on us and, as we had to take cover while the raid was on, it soon got a good hold. Rifle ammunition was also popping off every few minutes, so it became too dangerous to go near. When we found the engine and shafting were all right and that the steering gear seemed to work I decided to try to put to sea. We had no sooner started to heave away, when the aeroplanes came on us again and dropped bombs, one of which just missed the fore end of the bridge on the port side, stopped our gyro compass and shook the ship from stem to stern. The chief officer had left the windlass running and took cover under the forecastle head. When the raiders had passed, we tried our telemotor but found that it was broken, so we stopped the windlass. I called the engineers up and told them our position. It was hopeless to get aft to see if the steam gear was intact for no one could stay aft and steer owing to the fire and there was the danger that our spare ammunition in the tonnage opening would explode at any moment. Just as I suggested going aft (but was stopped by my chief officer) the first of the big shells went off.

With the fire in the after part of the ship burning out of control, and his steering gear out of action Captain Mackie now had to look to the safety of his crew, and he had little alternative but to order them to abandon ship. He signalled his intention and the minesweeper *Pangbourne* came alongside. He concludes his report:

> The chief and fifth engineers went below and drew the fires as much as possible. The natives would not go down below a second time. We mustered the natives and found only twenty-three on board, eight of whom belonged to the saloon, eight were engine-room men and seven were deck men, and there were also twelve European members of the crew. When we left the vessel she was burning fiercely aft.

Winston Churchill said of the Dunkirk evacuation, 'We must be very careful not to assign to this deliverance the attributes of a victory. Wars are not won by evacuations.' Nevertheless, for the British nation the deliverance of Dunkirk meant the difference between abject surrender and continued resistance. The cost, however, was considerable. When the final reckoning was made, it revealed that the BEF had lost 68,000 men, either dead, wounded or missing. It also left behind in France most of its equipment, more than 80,000 vehicles, including 445 tanks, 2,472 pieces of artillery, 165,000 tons of fuel, some 76,000 tons of ammunition, and 416,000 tons of stores.

In the course of the evacuation, 6 British and 3 French destroyers were lost, and 19 others damaged. Additionally, more than 200 British and Allied merchant ships of all types were sunk, and a similar number damaged. In the fight to keep the Luftwaffe away from the beaches, the RAF lost 145 aircraft, of which at least 42 were Hurricanes or Spitfires.

Operation DYNAMO was unprecedented in the history of modern warfare. Prior to the evacuation the official estimate of the number of men expected to be brought home ranged from 20,000 to 50,000. In the event, nearly 350,000 British, French and Belgian soldiers were lifted from the beaches of Dunkirk and transported back across the Channel to safety in the course of nine days. The evacuation was a magnificent example of the Royal Navy at its best. Backed by the determination and expertise of the merchant seamen and the enthusiasm of the men of the 'little ships', a miracle was indeed achieved. It was a miracle in which the *Clan Macalister* played a signifcant part. The landing craft she delivered to Dunkirk were responsible for the rescue of over 2,000 men, while the ship herself saved many others.

After being abandoned, the *Clan Macalister* sank on an even keel and came to rest on the bottom with her decks above water. Seen from the air, she appeared to be still afloat, and consequently for several days afterwards she continued to be a prime target for the Luftwaffe, thereby diverting their attention from other ships busy rescuing men. The Admiralty later estimated that she saved the loss of over a million pounds worth of other shipping. The total number of lives this unobtrusive Glasgow cargo liner was responsible for saving is incalculable.

In death, as in life, the *Clan Macalister* still exerts her influence on the port of Dunkirk, her burnt-out wreck lying on the bottom of the harbour, marked on the chart as a 'dangerous wreck' to be avoided by all who enter there.

CHAPTER THREE

Kretschmer Strikes

The miracle of Dunkirk was soon receding into history, eclipsed by the battle being raged in the skies above Britain. The stakes were high, the outcome still uncertain. Meanwhile, out in the broad Atlantic, tamed by the prevailing high pressure, the great ocean was at peace. Summer reigned in the Western Approaches, with light winds, calm seas, and a low undulating swell. A fitting welcome home for Blue Star's *Auckland Star*, thirty-two days out from Sydney, Australia, and inbound with nearly 11,000 tons of frozen meat, grain, steel and lead – a king's ransom to a nation at war.

Blue Star, along with so many of the 'big names' in British merchant shipping, is today no more than a fond memory kept alive by a handful of veterans who once sailed in its ships. The company was founded in 1911 by the Liverpool butchers Vesty Brothers who, dissatisfied with the high freight being charged to bring home frozen beef from their ranches in Argentina, decided the time was right to enter the world of shipping.

The Blue Star Line commenced trading in July 1911 with twelve second-hand ships, all with refrigerated holds, a venture which was immediately successful. When war broke out in 1914 all twelve vessels were snapped up by the Admiralty to supply the troops in France with frozen meat. The company prospered, and was able to contemplate acquiring new ships. The expansion continued between the wars and by 1939 Blue Star owned forty-one cargo liners, notable among them the twelve ships of the *Imperial Star* class, of which the *Auckland Star* was one. Built by Harland & Wolff in their Belfast shipyard and launched just at the outbreak of the Second World War, the 12,382-ton *Auckland Star* was commanded by 45-year-old Captain David Rattray MacFarlane, a New Zealander by birth, Scottish by heritage.

MacFarlane had joined Blue Star as a deck apprentice in 1910, and served as a watch-keeping officer throughout the First World War, running the gauntlet of enemy shot and shell until September 1917, when his ship was torpedoed and sunk by a U-boat. When war broke out again in 1939, he was in command of the *Imperial Star,* a four-year-old 17½-knotter of 10,733 tons. In early October 1939, the *Imperial Star* was crossing the Bay of Biscay homeward bound from Freetown, sailing alone, and zig-zagging at 16 knots, when she ran into trouble. Captain MacFarlane was called to the bridge by the Officer of the Watch. He later wrote in his report to the Admiralty:

> At 5 a.m. I sighted a convoy steaming practically on a parallel course to mine, 3–4 miles away on the starboard beam. We were called up by the guide ship, who asked us our name. We replied and he said something to the effect that 'You are shooting past us'. In the full daylight we recognised this ship as the s.s. *Yorkshire.*
>
> At about 6.45 a.m. we observed a small merchant vessel on the starboard bow. A few minutes later the look-out reported what he thought was a funnel on the horizon. On sighting this through telescopes, it appeared to be a small destroyer, and we thought that this destroyer was rounding up the merchant ships which had got out of the convoy during the night. As we could not see any mast, wireless or any superstructure other than what appeared to be the funnel we realised that this was a submarine. It was doing a very good speed through the water.
>
> The submarine was sighted very close to the steamer I mentioned before, steaming away from her, and I considered was acting very suspiciously as she turned away from the submarine, and then turned back again. The steamer was flying an ensign of some sort, which I could not recognise, the ship and the submarine being in the sun. The steamer was a small merchant ship with one funnel, two masts, the funnel being amidships. I do not think she was a British ship.
>
> The submarine made towards us. We went hard aport and put the submarine astern, and all hands went to stations. Flashes were seen to come from the fore part of the submarine, so we opened fire at 3000 yards, the shot falling short. We then put up to 6000 yards, and fired a second shot, which appeared to fall very close to

the submarine, and she dived. We then lost sight of the submarine, but she reappeared later on.

The submarine when she was firing was bearing 120° true. At 7.30 a.m. the submarine again appeared one point on the starboard quarter in the sun. At 7.45 a.m. the submarine was lost to sight and at 8 a.m we resumed our course.

The next morning, in position about 40 miles west of the Scilly Isles the 4th Officer sighted a periscope at 11.05 a.m. 5 points on the port bow within about ¾ of a mile. We immediately put the helm hard astarboard, rang telegraphs full ahead. We then went to action stations, and that was the last we saw of that submarine.

The convoy referred to by Captain MacFarlane was Convoy HG 3, which consisted of twenty-five merchantmen sailing northbound unescorted from Gibraltar. On 17 October, when midway across the Bay of Biscay, the convoy was set upon by three U-boats, *U-37*, *U-46* and *U-48*, who sank three ships, totalling 24,468 tons gross, including Bibby Line's cargo/passenger vessel *Yorkshire*, homeward bound from Rangoon with general cargo.

As dawn broke on 28 July 1940, the *Auckland Star* was some 90 miles south-west of Ireland and on course for the North Channel. Captain MacFarlane, on the bridge to see the sun come up, sniffed at the clean, salt-laden air and congratulated himself at yet another long voyage about to be successfully completed. But even though safety was at hand, he did not relax his vigilance. His gun's crew was closed up around the 4-inch on the poop, extra lookouts had been posted, and the *Auckland Star* was zig-zagging at her full 16½ knots, presenting a difficult target for any U-boat that might be lurking in her path.

As it happened, MacFarlane's caution was well founded. Right ahead, on the edge of the horizon, trimmed down so that only her conning tower was above water, was the Type VIIB *U-99*, commanded by the young *Kapitänleutnant* Otto Kretschmer, later to become Germany's top U-boat ace. Kretschmer was already on his way to fame, having in the first year of the war sunk fifteen Allied merchantmen, totalling over 50,000 tons gross. But those victories had not been won easily.

Leaving Kiel on her maiden war patrol in June 1940 for operations in the North Sea, *U-99* was unfortunate enough to be spotted on the surface by a reconnaissance seaplane from the battleship *Scharnhorst*, then patrolling in the area. There was no time for Kretschmer to identify his boat as friendly and the Arado pilot, sensing a quick kill, swooped on the U-boat, forcing her to crash dive. It was a very near miss, and a sobering experience, but *U-99* escaped with only superficial damage. Two days later, it happened again, the boat being caught on the surface by two German aircraft on patrol from Norway. In the mistaken belief that she was a British submarine, the aircraft subjected *U-99* to a combined attack that sent her limping back to Germany for repairs. Her first war patrol had lasted just eight days and had been a disappointing failure.

Kretschmer's bad luck continued into *U-99*'s second patrol. Sailing from Wilhelmshaven on 29 June to take up station off the south-west coast of Ireland, the submarine was again surprised while running on the surface. A Sunderland of Coastal Command came out of the sun unseen by *U-99*'s lookouts until it was almost overhead. At the last minute, Kretschmer cleared the conning tower and put the boat into a crash-dive. Unfortunately, *U-99* was then in shallow water and she hit the bottom with a thump that shook every rivet in her hull. However, the damage was not serious and she was repaired at sea.

U-99 then went on to sink six Allied merchantmen in succession, totalling 20,584 tons gross, and she captured another. It was the beginning of a very successful partnership between Otto Kretschmer and *U-99*, which was to endure for another eight months, and resulted in the sinking of another thirty-eight ships, including three British armed merchant cruisers. In recognition of his achievements Kretchsmer was raised to the rank of *Korvettenkapitän* (equivalent to Lieutenant Commander), and awarded the Knight's Cross with Oak Leaves and Crossed Swords.

When France surrendered in June 1940, Admiral Dönitz immediately moved his U-boats to the Biscay ports of Brest, La Pallice, Lorient and St. Nazaire, thus bringing them several hundred miles nearer to the Allied North Atlantic convoy routes and, perhaps more importantly, dispensing with the dangerous passage in and out via the north of Scotland. *U-99*, being now based in Lorient, was one of the first to enjoy this newly-won advantage when she sailed on her third war patrol on 25 July. The weather was also in her favour when she left Biscay, Kretschmer noting in his log 'Calm sea and long swell. Light breeze. Bright moonlight and cloudy.'

Being able to spend most of the time running on the surface, *U-99* made good speed, and as dawn approached on the 28th, she was off the south coast of Ireland in the vicinity of Cape Clear. This being the danger hour, Otto Kretschmer had joined the Watch Officer, *Leutnant* Heinrich Bargsten, in the conning tower. As the light strengthened, both officers and the two lookouts searched the horizon with their binoculars. But there was nothing in sight except a lonely seagull swooping low over the water in search of breakfast.

The horizon was hardening as the new day approached and, unwilling to risk being caught on the surface again by enemy planes, Kretschmer was considering going to periscope depth. He was about to give the order to clear the conning tower, when one of the lookouts reported sighting a ship on the port bow. Following the lookout's outstretched arm, Kretschmer swept the horizon with his binoculars and located the shadowy outline of a ship. In the growing light he examined her carefully. She appeared to be a merchant ship, but she was alone, looked to be very fast, and at least one gun was visible at her stern. In fact, she had all the appearances of a British armed merchant cruiser, a number of which were known to patrol these waters. Caution was needed. Kretschmer gave the order to trim down.

Captain MacFarlane, like all prudent shipmasters in those uncertain days, was also on the bridge to see the sun come up. This was the danger hour, half light, half dark, with the early morning haze confusing the horizon. With less than 15 hours to go to the safety of the North Channel, the *Auckland Star* was logging 16½ knots, but she was still vulnerable. MacFarlane had his crew at their action stations, with all guns manned, and was watchful of the morning shadows, any one of which might be hiding an enemy periscope.

Running with her casings awash, *U-99* was unseen in the half light, and Kretschmer's torpedo struck its target without warning. Fired at a range of 2,500 yards, it ran true, finding its mark in the *Auckland Star*'s hull midway between her Nos 5 and 6 holds.

The explosion was muted, but the ship gave a violent shudder, listed heavily over to port, and slowed to a halt as the sea poured into her broken hull. She began to settle by the stern.

It had all happened so fast that MacFarlane could do nothing to save his ship. A quick inspection below deck showed that both after holds were already flooded and the propeller shafts were fractured. Yet despite her grievous wounds the *Auckland Star* was reluctant to sink and half an hour later she was still afloat. Anxious to quit the scene, Kretchsmer closed in and launched another torpedo. This one hit the crippled ship squarely in her engine room, sending a tall geyser of smoke, water and debris soaring high in the air.

It seemed that the *Auckland Star*'s fate must be finally sealed, yet she still refused to go down. More than an hour had now elapsed since Kretchsmer had begun his attack, and he was aware his victim had transmitted an SOS, which had been acknowledged by a shore station. It was time to go, before the Royal Navy came looking for him, but before he left he fired a parting shot.

The *coup de grâce* struck forward of the *Auckland Star*'s bridge, and fifteen minutes later she rolled over to port, lifted her bows high in the air, and sank stern-first, leaving only a spreading patch of oil and debris, and four crowded lifeboats containing Captain David MacFarlane and his crew of seventy-three, to mark her passing. J. N. O'Driscoll, Able Seaman in the *Auckland Star*, kept a diary of events (times are GMT):

> Torpedoed 3.10 a.m. port quarter. Felt a terrific thud and shudder and saw a blinding flash. Collected a few odds and ends and took to the boats. 3.20 a.m. Second torpedo amidships just as we were pulling away at 4 a.m. approx. Port plates were flying in the air and streams of water also. Third torpedo sent amidships about 4.15 a.m. Submarine surfaced about 5 minutes afterwards to watch the gallant *Auckland Star* heel gracefully over on her port side and the bow rise in the air and then down by 4.45 a.m. Submarine moved off. SOS answered by Land's End almost immediately.

Seen from the other side of *U-99*'s periscope, the encounter was described in Terence Robertson's biography of Otto Kretchsmer,

The Golden Horseshoe, written with the full cooperation of Kretchsmer (published by Greenhill Books in 2003):

> At full speed *U-99* swept round towards the target in a large crescent movement that brought her into an attacking position by 5 a.m. When the range had closed to about one and a half miles, Kretchsmer shouted 'Fire one!' and the phosphorescent disturbance and the hiss of air in the empty tube marked the passage of the hurtling torpedo. In less than a minute there was a loud explosion at the stern of the target, and almost immediately Kassel intercepted the plain language call for help on the 600 metre band: 'Auckland Star torpedoed in position 52° 17′ N 12° 32′ W request help immediately'.
>
> Kretchsmer glanced anxiously to the east, there the first signs of dawn were appearing over the empty horizon. Then came the sudden whine of a shell overhead. Startled, Kretchsmer swung his glasses round on the stricken merchant. The crew were taking to the boats, but astern the gun's crew were firing at *U-99*, and the shooting was good. Not liking the idea of being holed, especially after the radio signal, Kretchsmer dived and decided to give her another torpedo. He looked again at the target through the periscope and saw the lifeboats pulling away from the *Auckland Star*. His orders came quickly, and a second torpedo left on its deadly mission. This time it was a direct hit between the bridge and funnel, but still she gave no sign of sinking. Angrily, Kretchsmer fired a third torpedo and scored his third hit in the same place as the second. The *Auckland Star* rose in the water and turned slowly and reluctantly over on her side, finally capsizing.
>
> Few minutes later lookout spotted a periscope. Kretchsmer altered course to put the small silhouette of their stern to the enemy, when two loud explosions came from the opposite side. These torpedoes were fired by the British submarine which had missed and rendered themselves harmless.

There is no record of any British submarine being in the area at the time, and it is more than likely that the attacker was another U-boat, which failed to report this incident of 'friendly fire'.

Now that the *Auckland Star* had finally sunk, Kretchsmer was anxious to clear the scene as quickly as possible. As a precaution against the imminent arrival of Allied aircraft in answer to MacFarlane's SOS, he decided to remain submerged and move to the east in search of another victim. Running at slow speed on her electric motors *U-99* remained at periscope level throughout the hours of daylight and, it being high summer, the sun was reluctant to drop below the horizon. This it finally did at about 2000 hrs. Another hour of summer twilight followed, and it was after 2100 hrs before Kretchsmer deemed it safe to surface. It was a fine, warm night, and motoring on the surface was not unpleasant, but much to Kretchsmer's frustration, the night was also empty. It was not until the very early hours of the 29th before the first sighting was made and, like the *Auckland Star*, this vessel was also a 'gauntlet runner', another fast British cargo liner sailing alone.

The 7,336-ton *Clan Menzies*, a twin-screw 17½-knotter, under the command of Captain William Hughes, was also nearing the end of the long passage from Australia. She had on board a cargo consisting of 4,000 tons of wheat and grain, 2,000 tons dried fruit, 1,500 tons zinc, and 840 tons general, all consigned to Liverpool.

As he closed the stranger, Kretchsmer identified her as a Clan liner by her conspicuous heavy-lift derricks and, as she was deep in the water, a target worthy of his attention. Ordering full speed, he manouevred to get ahead of her, which although the British ship was zig-zagging, took a full two hours. It was beginning to get light before *U-99* was in position, about 2 miles off the starboard bow of the *Clan Menzies* and ready to attack.

Kretchsmer's first torpedo either missed or failed to detonate and the *Clan Menzies* continued on her way, oblivious to the fact that she was under attack. His second torpedo, however, ran true, blasting a great hole in the Clan liner's hull in way of her engine room through which the sea poured, flooding her engine spaces and bringing her to a halt. The entire watch in the engine room, two engineer officers and four ratings were killed by the blast. On deck, both starboard lifeboats were reduced to matchwood, and the wireless room, along with all its equipment, was wrecked before a distress message could be sent.

The *Clan Menzies* settled rapidly by the stern, but before she sank, Captain Hughes and the remaining eighty-seven members of his crew abandoned ship in the two undamaged lifeboats. One boat made a landfall on the coast of County Sligo, while the other was picked up by the Limerick Steamship Company's *Kyleclare* two days later.

His appetite whetted, Otto Kretschmer moved to the east, and in the early hours of 31 July *U-99* was 40 miles south-west of Barra Head when she met up with another fast runner. She was the 5,745-ton fruit carrier *Jamaica Progress*, homeward from the West Indies with bananas. Sailing unescorted, her speed her only defence, the Kingston-registered ship was easy meat for Kretschmer, who all but blew her stern off. Her propeller shaft was broken, both her masts were split and her wireless aerials brought down. She began to go down by the stern with a rush. Eight men lost their lives, while the remaining forty-seven of the crew of the *Jamaica Progress* took to the boats, one of which was picked up by a British trawler, the other coming ashore in the Outer Hebrides.

Kretschmer's cup was full when, twelve hours later, the west-bound convoy OB 21 was sighted. Choosing one of the outriders, the 6,322-ton British tramp *Jersey City*, he closed in and hit her with a torpedo just abaft her engine room. She broke in two and sank one and a half hours later. Two of her crew lost their lives.

U-99 was heavily depth charged by the convoy escorts, but escaped unscathed, returning that night to torpedo the 10,000-ton Norwegian tanker *Strinda*. The damaged tanker was able to make port under her own steam. *U-99* again came under heavy attack but, unpeturbed, Kretschmer returned three hours later to attack another tanker. The 6,556-ton, Liverpool-registered *Lucerna* was, like the *Strinda*, sailing in ballast, and although Kretschmer's torpedo blew a hole 35ft by 18ft in her hull, she remained afloat. Kretschmer surfaced and attempted to sink her by gunfire, but again failed. The *Lucerna* also made port.

U-99 was now in the middle of the convoy and, unseen by the escorts, Kretschmer took advantage of the confusion he had caused by torpedoing Anglo Saxon's 8,016-ton *Alexia*, another ballasted tanker. Her Chinese crew panicked and took to the boats, but her Captain and his officers stayed aboard. When *U-99* surfaced and opened fire on the damaged ship, the *Alexia*'s 4-inch armament hit back with such accuracy that Kretschmer was forced to crash-dive. *Alexia* was able to return to port for repairs.

The attack on Convoy OB 21 had not been a huge success, but in the space of five days *U-99* had sunk four ships, totalling 32,345 gross tons, bringing Otto Kretschmer's grand total to 117,637 tons. In recognition of this, he was awarded the Knight Insignia of the Iron Cross when the boat arrived back in Lorient.

By this time, the survivors of the *Auckland Star* had also made a landfall in neutral Ireland. Able Seaman O'Driscoll's diary continues:

> We are 64 miles off the south-west coast of Ireland. Sails put up 5.15 a.m. We were last boat to leave. Captain MacFarlane came in our boat but transferred to No.1 boat just afterwards. He looked all in. Everybody acted just as if we were changing watches! Captain was as cool as a cucumber, magnificent. The only injury was a cut cheek to Greaser Joe Blain, one of the poop lookouts, a Sunderland flying boat appeared at 7.55 a.m. and circled round until 9.30 a.m. Biscuits and brandy once or twice during morning, dinner at 1 p.m. It was corned beef and biscuits with water.
>
> Another flying boat circled around us at 2 p.m. – plane landed at 2.20 p.m. Rowed like hell towards her, sails as well! Pilot made for Captain's boat and away again by 2.35 p.m. A destroyer is supposed to be coming out this evening. An Irish coaster passed us at 4 p.m. But did not take any notice of us! Bailing out while rowing. Tins of milk and biscuits passed around. Brandy again, too, three of four boats still together at 1.50 a.m.
>
> 29/7/40: Slept on oars fore and aft. Not a bad bed when you are tired but rather cold. Bailing out again at 3 a.m. and brandy passed around. Had a good swig. We are going to make our own way in. Fine morning again. We have now been in the boats 24 hours and it is 25 hours since we caught the unlikely blow. Still, thank God for our lives. Still wisecracking – 'I think I will have ham and eggs or a steak, and what no tea?' All in good spirits. Instead we get biscuits, bully beef, skimmed

milk and water. My atlas is being used by Captain and his Mate – good old sixpenny atlas. Sighted land about 1 p.m. and changed course.

30/7/40: Been rowing nearly all night, land coming slowly nearer. Flares used but no success. Time now 5.30 a.m. and 50 hours in boats. No sign of 1st Mate's boat since 1 p.m. Yesterday. At 8 a.m. little fishing boats off Blasket Islands came out to see if they could assist. Captain asked them to get a motor boat to tow us in. At 9.50 a.m. a fishing boat D 167 came to us – at last! First Mate's boat has not turned up yet. Passed kettle of tea and bread from boat to boat. Landed Dingle 12.45 p.m.

Dingle, in 1940 the only town of any significant size on the south-west coast of Ireland, was a sleepy market town which saw little activity other than a monthly sheep and cattle auction. Not surprisingly, the sudden arrival on its shores of three boatloads of British merchant seamen, survivors of a torpedoed ship, created a considerable stir. O'Driscoll's description of their reception reads like the script of a Hollywood musical comedy:

Whole town turned out on wharf. Marched through the streets – with flags given to us by people – towards the police barracks. Taken in back entrance of pub – drinks given. Fifty-seven hours in boats. Went to church and gave my thanks to Almighty God and then went to presbytery and asked the priest to hear confession, which he did. Gave up brandy and tobacco. I got my atlas back from the Captain and fitted out with complete outfits. Free cigarettes and drinks, meals and bed. Absolute freedom of the town and really good-hearted people. I hope advantage is not taken of them. Understand Mate's boat picked up late afternoon off Clifton Galway, 80 miles up the coast. Roll call at the barracks and return of identity cards.

31/7/40: Not had a cigarette this morning – free drinks at Murphy's. Went to Guard House and put my belongings in a sack. Report to barracks at 12 a.m. and special buses for us. Captain given a rousing cheer and 'for he's a jolly good fellow'. Left Dingle 12.30 p.m. And caught 2 p.m. train to Dublin.

After a brief spell of survivor's leave, David MacFarlane assumed command of the *Melbourne Star*, another of Blue Star's *Imperial* class. When, in July 1941 the call came to relieve the besieged island of Malta, he was to be found as Convoy Commodore of the six merchantmen that formed Operation SUBSTANCE.

CHAPTER FOUR

Under the Southern Cross

August is not the best month in the Tasman Sea. The southern winter is enjoying its last fling, with overcast skies, a shrieking sou'wester carrying with it the chill of Antarctica and blinding rain squalls. August 1940 was no exception. In fact, it was then little different to the North Atlantic in dreary November. So thought Captain James Laird as the rain sheeted down on the *Turakina* once again, reducing visibility to zero.

The 9,691-ton *Turakina*, built on the Clyde in 1923 for the New Zealand Shipping Company of London, had already loaded 4,000 tons of wheat, lead and dried fruit in Australian ports, and was crossing the Tasman Sea to Wellington, where she would complete her cargo with frozen New Zealand lamb. Then she faced the return voyage to Britain via the Panama Canal, which at her best speed of 13 knots would take her some five weeks. It was a long haul, but to those who manned the *Turakina*, an all-British crew of fifty-seven led by 45-year-old Captain James Boyd Laird, it presented no hardship.

Laird, a fiery Glaswegian, often fondly referred to as 'Jock' was a shipmaster of considerable experience, having first gone to sea in 1910 at the age of 15. He had served throughout the First World War, firstly in merchant ships, then as a Royal Naval Reservist. He joined the New Zealand Shipping Company when the war finished in 1918. The Company owed its existence to Captain James Cook, who in 1773 brought the first sheep from the Cape of Good Hope to New Zealand in his barque *Endeavour*. Four of the flock of six died on the long voyage across the Indian Ocean, the two surviving animals being landed in Queen Charlotte Sound. They also died three days later, but this initial move to stimulate the colony's economy encouraged others to try. By 1894, New Zealand's vast alpine grasslands were supporting five million sheep.

The exportation of wool, mainly to Britain, began in 1873 with the foundation in Wellington of the New Zealand Shipping

Company by a group of ex-patriate sheep farmers. Beginning with four second-hand sailing ships, the company prospered and within four years was operating a fleet of seventeen steamers, with a number of others on charter. In 1882, NZS, which had by then moved its headquarters to London, installed refrigeration in its ships and began the export of frozen lamb from Australia and New Zealand to Europe. The new venture was a huge success and by the time the First World War began in 1914, NZS was running regular service with thirty-two vessels between Europe and the Antipodes, carrying general cargo outward and returning with frozen lamb and wool. The company lost nine ships in the conflict, but a post-war building programme soon restored the fleet and by 1939 thirty-six fast cargo liners were sailing under the New Zealand Shipping Company's colours, all registered in London and manned by British crews.

When the *Turakina* entered the rain squall in the Tasman Sea it was late afternoon, with only a few hours left to sunset – and this could not come soon enough for Captain Laird. The Japanese attack on Pearl Harbor was more than a year away and peace still reigned in these distant waters, but there had been talk in Sydney of a German commerce raider at large which had already sunk several Allied merchantmen. The *Turakina* mounted a 4.7-inch anti-submarine gun on her poop and was equipped with several machine-guns for defence against aircraft, but as trained naval gunners were in short supply when she sailed from the UK, the manning and maintenance of these guns was left to Captain Laird's discretion. He had chosen seven deck ratings, to be led by Third Officer Mallett, who at the behest of the Ministry had attended a three-day gunnery course held in a dockside warehouse, where time-served naval petty officers explained the virtues of the antique weapons being fitted to merchant ships of the day. Mallett had come away somewhat confused, but bearing a certificate stating that he was competent in the firing and maintenance of anything from a .38 revolver to a 6-inch breech loader. However, backed by Captain Laird, Mallett had trained his men hard on the outward voyage and by the time they reached Australian waters they were passable shots with the *Turakina's* 4.7-inch and able to put up a fair AA barrage with her various machine guns. In the absence of trained DEMS gunners, then in short supply, they would have to do.

When the *Turakina* emerged from the rain squall, it was as if a curtain had been suddenly drawn aside. A weak sun glinted on the newly sluiced decks and the horizon was once more hard. The sudden clearance also revealed a ship on the port bow, bearing down on them.

Captain Laird ran his binoculars over the newcomer. She was obviously a neutral, as she was still painted in her company colours, black hull, white upperworks, black funnel with two white bands. Probably Japanese. It was not unusual to meet Japanese ships in these waters and Laird turned his attention elsewhere. As he did so, gun crews aboard the German commerce raider *Orion*, masquerading as OSK Line's *Tokyo Maru*, closed the breeches of their 5.9s.

In the First World War, the British 'Q' ships, requisitioned merchantmen armed and manned by the Royal Navy, had proved to be a great success, being responsible for sinking a number of U-boats. Not to be outdone, the German Navy had taken up the idea, using mainly fast converted cargo liners armed with guns hidden by drop-down shutters. Preying on Allied cargo liners sailing alone in the more remote corners of the oceans, the German commerce raiders had sunk or captured some 340,000 tons of shipping. The idea was revived when war broke out again in 1939, nine fast cargo liners being taken up for conversion to commerce raiders. First to be commissioned was the *Hilfskreuzer Orion*.

Launched in Hamburg in 1930 for Hamburg-Amerika Line, the 7,021-ton *Kurmark* was a single-screw, steam turbine vessel with a service speed of 15 knots, ideally suited for the role the German Admiralty had in mind. She was requisitioned in 1939, her accommodation was stripped out and rebuilt to house a naval crew of 350, and she was armed with six 5.9-inch, one 3-inch, six smaller calibre AA guns, and six 21-inch torpedo tubes. She also carried, as a reconnaissance aid, an Arado Ar 196 spotter plane. Officially designated as Hilfskreuzer (Auxiliary Cruiser) 36, the *Kurmark* was renamed *Orion* on being commissioned into the German Navy.

Disguised as the Greek steamer *Rokos*, and under the command of *Korvettenkapitän* Kurt Weyher, the *Orion* sailed from Germany on her maiden operational voyage on 6 April 1940. Passing to the north of Iceland to avoid British patrols, she broke out into the

Atlantic through the Denmark Strait under the cover of fog and sleet a few days later. Heading south, she encountered her first victim, the 5,207-ton *Haxby*, at dawn on 24 April. It was then that Weyher learned that tackling a British tramp was not the walkover he had anticipated.

The *Haxby*, owned by the Ropner Shipping Company of South Shields and commanded by Captain Cornelius Arundel, was sailing alone on passage from Glasgow to Corpus Christie, Texas, where she was to load a cargo of scrap metal. Weyher put a shot across her bows, fully expecting the British ship to stop and surrender. Captain Arundel, however, refused to bend the knee. Putting his helm hard over, he presented his stern to the German raider, rang for emergency full speed, ordered his 4-inch gun's crew to open fire, and sent word to the radio room to transmit the RRR signal.

On a good day with a following wind, the best the *Haxby* could manage was 10 knots, but with the *Orion* lobbing shells after her, the Ropner tramp ran for the horizon like a startled rabbit, the ancient 4-inch at her stern spitting defiance. The chase was short and bloody. The *Orion* quickly narrowed the gap and, anxious to stem the *Haxby's* frantic calls for help, *Korvettenkapitän* Weyher ordered his gunners to concentrate their fire on the fleeing tramp's radio room. The wooden house abaft the *Haxby's* bridge was set on fire and First Radio Officer Sidney Jones was killed at his key. As the *Haxby's* transmitter fell silent, the German gunners shifted their fire to her bridge, completely demolishing it with seventy rounds of 5.9. The *Haxby's* scuppers ran red with blood.

Weyher did not give the order to cease fire until the *Haxby* had stopped and lowered her boats and it was obvious she would offer no more resistance. By then, the British ship was on fire from end to end and sixteen of her crew lay dead upon her decks. But although she was holed below the waterline and low in the water, the tough old tramp refused to sink. In desperation, Weyher was forced to use a torpedo to send her to the bottom. The twenty-four men who survived the gun battle, including Captain Arundel, were picked up by the *Orion* and would eventually end up in a prisoner of war camp in Germany.

Still smarting from his first encounter with a British merchantman, Weyher continued south, rounded Cape Horn, and set a course for New Zealand. He laid mines in the approaches to Auckland in accordance with his orders, then moved north. On 18 June, the *Orion* was 600 miles north-east of Auckland and casting her net amongst the Pacific islands, when she sighted her next potential victim. She was the 5,781-ton *Tropic Sea*, a Norwegian steamer commanded by Captain Henrik Nicolaysen, on passage from Australia to New York via Panama, with 8,000 tons of wheat. The following is an extract from the report of an inquiry held at Gibraltar in September 1940:

> Captain Nicolaysen says they sighted a large steamer on the starboard bow at 7 a.m. on June 18, and at 10.30, when in position 28-04S 166-40W, the ship was abreast 1 to 1½ miles off. The Captain was below, but upon hearing the shot fired across their bows he ran upon the bridge, where the 3rd Mate was on watch. Tropic Sea was proceeding at a greater speed than the other vessel and was about to overtake it, but Orion increased her speed and when another two shots were fired, Captain Nicolaysen decided to stop the engines. A signal was hoisted on the raider telling them to refrain from using the wireless. The Captain ordered both amidships lifeboats to be lowered. He noticed that the raider was also preparing to launch a boat, but when she manoeuvered astern of the Tropic Sea he decided to take the ship's papers over to the raider in the starboard lifeboat. Halfway, he met the raider's boat, and was ordered to return to his ship, however, this order was changed and he was sent over to the Orion, where he was told to go into the saloon where the papers were examined by Weyher and his officers. Upon finding that the cargo had been shipped from an Australian port and was to be delivered at New York to the order of the Commonwealth Bank, they told the Captain he would have to stay on board for about four days, because they had to communicate with Germany to find out what to do with the ship and cargo. The 1st and 2nd Mates, the 1st Engineer and 11 crew were also to come on board, and they were all locked up in the hold . . .

The above may appear to be irrelevant, but it goes a long way towards illustrating the marked difference in reaction by British and Norwegian merchant ships when threatened by a commerce raider. Whereas, in the case of the *Haxby*, Captain Arundel had chosen to fight and run, thereby losing the lives of sixteen of his crew, Captain Nicolaysen had offered immediate surrender, with the result that he and his men survived. Who is to judge which man was right? But, then, wars are not won by appeasement.

The *Tropic Sea* was sent home under the German flag with a German prize crew and fifty-five British and Norwegian prisoners on board, but when she was within twenty-four hours of reaching her destination, the Biscay port of Bordeaux, she was intercepted by the Royal Navy. Rather than allow her to fall into enemy hands, her prize crew scuttled her. All on board were rescued.

Meanwhile, the *Orion* had roamed the length and breadth of the Tasman Sea searching for more conquests, but for two months she searched in vain. It was halfway through August before she chanced upon the small French inter-island steamer *Notou*. The *Notou*'s best speed was only 8 knots and she quickly succumbed to the raider's guns. At this point, disgusted by the dearth of shipping in the area, *Korvettenkapitän* Weyher was considering moving to fresh pastures in the Indian Ocean, when to his great delight the *Turakina* emerged from the rain squall. Ordinary Seaman Ted Sweeny, who was keeping lookout on the bridge of the *Turakina*, described what followed:

> We met the raider at 4.15 p.m. approaching on the port bow. I was on stand-by on the bridge at the time. The raider swung round to the starboard side, went round our stern and came to a position on our port beam. The Captain, who was conferring with the Chief Officer, changed course as the raider started to signal. The Captain then ordered 'Action Stations'.
>
> The raider fired and our Captain ordered us to return this fire, this was about 6 p.m. Our gun was served by the following members of the crew: Perry, McGowan, Norton, Foster, Quinn, Manders, Burgess and Taylor, who was attending to the bridge telephone.

It is on record that Captain Laird had once sworn he would fight his ship to the last if ever she were attacked by the enemy and now he was true to his word. Ringing for full emergency speed, he put the helm hard over and the *Turakina* heeled as she came around in a tight circle to present her stern to the raider. As he was zig-zagging away from the danger, Laird instructed First Radio Officer to send out the QQQ (I am being attacked by an enemy merchant raider) signal. As the first plaintive notes of the distress call went out over the ether, *Orion* opened fire with her 5.9s, aiming for the *Turakina's* wireless aerial. Laird ordered his gun's crew to fire back and the 4-inch on her poop barked defiance.

The range was now down to about 2½ miles, unmissable for the *Orion's* trained naval gunners, even though they were firing over open sights. Their first salvo brought down the *Turakina's* fore topmast, and with it her wireless aerial and the crow's nest complete with the lookout man, who was very gravely injured when he crashed to the deck. The German gunners then concentrated their fire on the *Turakina's* bridge, which they reduced to a burning shambles in a matter of minutes. The accommodation abaft the bridge was next in line of fire and was soon ablaze. All communication between the bridge and the after gun platform had been cut off, but the *Turakina's* scratch gun's crew continued to fire back. At least one of their shells scored a direct hit on the *Orion*, causing considerable damage and wounding a number of her crew.

The running gunfight went on for more than half an hour, at the end of which the *Turakina* was reduced to a burning wreck, her decks littered with the dead and dying. Weyher finally lost patience, closed to within 1,500 yards and launched a torpedo. His frustration was increased when the torpedo porpoised in the heavy swell and hit the *Turakina* in the stern, rather than in the engine room at which it was aimed. No serious damage was caused, but that was hardly necessary as, in Weyher's words, 'she burns like a blazing torch'. Stubbornly, the British liner still showed no sign of sinking, but Captain Laird had come to the conclusion that there was no way he could win this fight. He rang the engines to stop and ordered those who were still alive to take to the boats.

The *Turakina's* two port side lifeboats had been destroyed by gunfire, but her two starboard boats were still intact. One of these was successfully launched with fourteen men on board, seven of whom were wounded, but as they were lowering the other boat, which also had wounded on board, a second torpedo slammed into the *Turakina*. With her back broken, she sank two minutes later. Luckily, the first boat had already cleared the ship's side, but the other was still alongside, and felt the full blast of the exploding torpedo. Only seven of the boat's occupants survived to be taken on board the *Orion*, where they joined the crew of the other boat. When a head count was made, it revealed that Captain James Laird and thirty-three of his men had gone down with the *Turakina*.

Ordinary Seaman Edward Sweeny later gave his version of the action:

> I went down for my life-jacket at this time (when the *Orion* was first sighted) and when I returned a shell hit the foremast. There was no confusion on board. Firing was going on all the time and the action lasted for about three quarters of an hour. Probably the second shell hit our wireless room, seriously wounding the operator, who was continuously sending out signals. There was a lot of damage to the engineers' accommodation, where the Sixth Engineer was killed. The two lifeboats on the port side were destroyed.
>
> A shell hit the funnel and the vessel caught fire. The Chief Officer ordered us to fire stations. The ship was also hit in No.2 hold. The third or fourth shell fired at us hit the bridge and killed Able Seaman Gorman. The Captain came out of his cabin, his face was bleeding, and he ordered us to take to the lifeboats, two of which on the starboard side were undamaged. The Captain also instructed that the guns be kept firing, but this was not possible as the available ammunition was exhausted, owing to the ammunition column being sent to fire stations.

It had been a hopelessly one-sided contest: the *Orion*'s battery of six 5.9s manned by trained naval gunners, versus the *Turakina*'s single 1918-vintage 4-inch manned by a crew of rank amateurs. Captain Laird had sworn to fight to the last and he was true to his word. However, with the range down to 2½ miles, he was fighting in vain. The *Turakina*'s bridge was a flaming ruin, all communication with the rest of the ship was down, much of the accommodation was on fire, two of the four lifeboats were wrecked and many of the crew dead or dying.

In the course of the furious battle, only one shell from the *Turakina's* 4-inch had hit the *Orion*, but it had caused much damage. For *Korvettenkapitän* Weyher this was the last straw and he decided to finish the matter with torpedoes. By then Captain Laird had accepted defeat, and ordered his surviving crew to take to the boats. Ted Sweeny takes up the story again:

> As Quin and I boarded the aft lifeboat a shell hit the funnel. At this time the vessel was very low in the water and was still moving and burning fiercely. The raider's guns were firing continuously.
>
> When we were some distance away two torpedoes struck our vessel and the explosion which followed sank our second lifeboat which had been launched in the meantime. There were three survivors of about 30 crew who were in this lifeboat. As my boat was drifting we picked up three men from the water, making a total of 17 on board.
>
> Fourth Officer Spencer was in charge of our lifeboat and as there was a dying man and others wounded in the boat he flashed his torch and we were picked up by the raider. It was very wet and rough by this time and when we boarded the raider we were given tea and told we were good shots. It was seen that the damage had been done to the camouflaged deck houses and we were informed that we had several near misses. We were also given blankets and sleeping accommodation.
>
> In the morning we were told that Manders (Ordinary Seaman Sydney Mander) had died. We met Engineer Slater, Third Officer Mallett and Burgess, who had been picked up by the raider's boat. The Third Officer informed us that the Captain, Chief Officer, Chief Engineer, Second Engineer and several others were standing at No.5 hatch when the torpedoes struck the ship. They were not seen again.
>
> From the time the lifeboat left the *Turakina* until we were picked up by the raider a period of three to four hours had passed.

While the *Turakina* was being pounded into a blazing wreck, First Radio Officer Sydney Jones remained at his key transmitting the QQQ distress call, followed by the ship's name and position. His dogged perseverance paid off, for his calls for help were heard by the light cruiser HMNZS *Achilles*, of River Plate fame, which was then alongside in Wellington. She immediately began to raise steam and late that night sailed to the *Turakina*'s rescue. The cruiser was joined by a flying boat from Auckland next morning and an extensive sea and air search was begun in the vicinity of the *Turakina*'s reported position. Later in the day, the Australian cruiser HMAS *Perth* and another aircraft also combed the area, but nothing was seen of the British ship or her attacker. *Achilles* continued to search for another forty-eight hours, but found no trace of either ship. The *Turakina* had gone to the bottom taking Captain James Laird and thirty-five of his men with her, leaving not even a scrap of debris to mark her passing. The commerce raider *Orion*, having taken prisoner the surviving twenty-one men of the *Turakina*'s crew, had made off to the south-west in steadily deteriorating weather, shrouded by poor visibility.

Ordinary Seaman Ted Sweeny later commented:

Our attackers praised our courage for fighting against overwhelming odds, but considered us 'mad English'. I was rescued by our attackers and eight months later, after being imprisoned on another German ship, the *Altmark*, we safely docked in Bordeaux, France. I had no money or belongings as everything went down with the ship.

After imprisonment in a transit camp, we were eventually entrained for Germany. Although armed guards were in our carriage, I escaped by diving from the train 20 miles from Paris, in occupied France. After some hair-raising experiences, I escaped from a concentration camp in Argelès-sur-Mer, Southern France. I crossed the Pyrenees into Spain, and was arrested and jailed by the Civil Guard for not having papers to prove my identity. After a spell in filthy jails, I was imprisoned in a labour concentration camp at Miranda de Ebro, in Northern Spain, carrying a large basket of stones on my back, helping to build a new major road.

Fifteen months after leaving England, I was eventually released, reaching Glasgow via Gibraltar, none the worse for my adventures. Apart from a newly shaven head just before we left, I was quite fit, and glad to be back home in familiar normal circumstances.

In 1941, the following appeared in the *London Gazette*:

> Third Officer Mallett was the gunnery officer and his splendid example of courage and determination inspired the gun's crew. Later when the chief radio officer was blown from his post, he went to his rescue and carried him down to the boat. Chief Radio Officer Jones displayed great courage and devotion to duty, thereby sacrificing his life. He remained on board to send out distress messages until he was blown from his desk through a wooden bulkhead. Able Seaman McGowan displayed conspicuous bravery and a high sense of duty while serving the guns throughout the action.

Five days after meeting and sinking the *Turakina*, at noon on 25 August, the *Orion* was to be found sheltering in the snow storms of the Great Southern Ocean some 200 miles south of Tasmania. Cold and windswept, completely devoid of other shipping, this was not a good place to linger, and by then satsified that he had shaken off all pursuit, *Korvettenkapitän* Weyher decided to try his luck further to the north and west. Crossing the Australian Bight, he trawled the shipping lanes, but he had no luck here either. Furthermore, the weather was even worse than in the sub-Antarctic region to the south. It was marginally warmer, but rain squalls were seriously reducing visibility and, beam-on to the long, rolling swell of the Bight, the raider was rolling so heavily that at times she was dipping her bulwarks under.

Steaming doggedly to the west, *Orion* finally rounded Cape Leuwin and entered the comparative calm of the Indian Ocean. For the next five days she criss-crossed the route to the Cape of Good Hope, but still the horizon remained stubbornly empty of Allied shipping. Weyher reported the situation to Berlin, who instructed him to return to the Tasman Sea, where a rendezvous would be arranged with a Japanese supply ship. With food, water and fuel restocked, *Orion* was to move to the Japanese-occupied Marshall Islands in the Pacific, where her machinery would be given along overdue refit.

On the passage eastwards the weather was no better and *Orion* had to endure another eight days of heavy rolling in the Australian Bight. When she reached the Pacific, her orders were changed and, after idling for almost three weeks, she made a rendezvous with her sister raider *Komet* and the supply vessel *Kulmerland*. After restocking from the latter *Orion* joined forces with *Komet,* and over the next three months the two raiders sank seven Allied merchantmen, including New Zealand Shipping Company's 16,712-ton cargo/passenger liner *Rangitane*. The liner, which was fully loaded with frozen meat and wool for British ports, had on board 111 passengers, including thirty-six women. When attacked, she defended herself while trying to run away, but the *Orion* outgunned her and five of the *Rangitane's* crew and five passengers were killed in the protracted exchange of fire. Weyher eventually sank the liner with torpedoes.

Orion and *Komet* went their separate ways in January 1941, *Orion* moving into the Indian Ocean, where she spent the next six months chasing shadows. She had by then been sixteen months continuously at sea and her engines were giving trouble. Furthermore, not having seen action for six months, the morale of her crew, officers and men, was at low ebb. Weyher requested permission to return home, which was granted.

On 29 July *Orion* was on her way north, passing west of the Cape Verde Islands, when shortly before sunset on 29 July she encountered the South American Saint Line's 5,792-ton steamer *Chaucer*, bound for Buenos Aires in ballast. The British ship was challenged and ordered to stop, but her Master, Captain Charles Bradley, refused to comply, and in time-honoured style presented his stern to the raider and ran.

A fierce running gun battle ensued, in which Bradley used his single 4-inch to good effect, but against the *Orion's* 5.9s it was a hopeless contest for the British ship. She was hit in the engine room, set on fire, and her 4-inch was blown off her stern with a direct hit. Up to that point the *Chaucer* had miraculously incurred no casualties and Captain Bradley decided to surrender while that held good. He stopped his ship, lowered his boats, and all forty-eight crew abandoned ship and were taken prisoner. The *Chaucer* was then sunk by torpedoes and gunfire.

The *Orion,* her engines failing, finally limped into Bordeaux in mid-August 1941, having sailed over 125,000 miles and accounted for 73,000 tons of Allied merchant shipping. Her voyage had been a commendable achievement, but hardly a huge success when compared with the average U-boat sinkings. She saw no further active service, being banished to the Baltic as a training ship. On 4 May 1945, with the end of the war in Europe in sight, the ex-commerce raider *Orion* was engaged in evacuating German service personnel ahead of the advancing Russian army, when she was bombed and set on fire. She was eventually beached, but of the 4,000 on board, only 150 survived.

CHAPTER FIVE

Slaughter in the Indian Ocean

1925 was the year of the 'Bright Young Things' and the Charleston, a time of long-awaited indulgence. The horrors of the Great War of 1914–18 were still fresh in everyone's mind, but the depression that followed the war was past history, and the sunlight beckoned. No one would have predicted that, in less than a decade and a half, the nations of Europe would be at each other's throats again. Not least Sir George Hunter, watching proudly as the latest product of the Swan Hunter yard slipped her chains and slid gracefully down the slipway to wet her keel in the River Tyne.

At 9,557 tons gross, the twin-screw motor tanker *Athelking*, built for the growing fleet of the British Molasses Company, later to become Athel Line of London, was one of the biggest and best of her day. She was destined for the oil trade centred on the Caribbean to carry either molasses or fuel oil as required. In the years between the wars she would span the oceans, earning her keep, and much more.

Fifteen years after her launch, on 9 September 1940, the *Athelking* was some 270 miles south-east of Rodriguez Island, in the Southern Indian Ocean, bound from Sydney to East Africa in ballast. She was alone in an empty ocean, with only the occasional passing rain squall to mar the horizon. Far to the north-west in the North Atlantic, Hitler's U-boats were tearing great holes in Britain's vital sea lanes, but here, as the turbulent south-west monsoon drew to a close, peace still reigned.

Commanded by 41-year-old Captain Albert Tomkins, the *Athelking* carried a British crew of forty-three and was conventionally armed with a 4-inch anti-submarine gun mounted aft, plus various calibre machine-guns for defence against aircraft. It seemed highly unlikely at the time that any guns would be needed in the Indian Ocean, as no enemy presence had yet been reported in these waters. In fact, this not being the busiest of shipping lanes, Captain Tomkins was surprised when the lookout reported a ship overtaking on the port quarter. He moved to the after end of the bridge and focused his binoculars on the stranger. She was overhauling the *Athelking* at a fast rate, and as she drew nearer Tomkins was able to make out her black-painted hull and black funnel with two pale blue bands, with the Norwegian ensign at her stern. One of Wilhelmsen's fast Far East traders. No threat there.

In fact, though the overtaking ship appeared to be a harmless unarmed neutral, she was actually a German raider painted up to look like one of Wilhelmsen's, and armed to the teeth with guns hidden behind drop-down shutters. The 7,862-ton *Atlantis*, ex-*Goldenfels* of the Hansa Line, was the first of Germany's merchant raiders to reach the Indian Ocean. Commanded by *Korvettenkapitän* Bernhard Rogge, and manned by a naval crew of 400, the *Atlantis* was a force to be reckoned with. Her main armament consisted of six rapid-fire 5.9-inch guns (albeit recycled from the 1906 vintage battleship *Schlesien*), one 3-inch bow-chaser, two 37mm and four 20mm AA guns, plus four 21-inch torpedo tubes with twenty-four torpedoes. She also carried 92 mines and two Heinkel He-114 reconnaissance seaplanes.

The *Atlantis* sailed from Kiel on 11 March 1940, but was delayed by unseasonable ice in the Baltic, and it was another month before she reached the Denmark Strait and broke out into the Atlantic. Disguised as the Japanese steamer *Kasii Maru*, she headed south for the Cape of Good Hope, sinking the British merchantman *Scientist* on 3 May. The *Scientist*, one of T. & J. Harrison's of Liverpool homeward from the Indian coast with jute and ore, bolted for the horizon when challenged, thus setting a pattern Rogge would become accustomed to. She was stopped and set on fire, her crew taking to the boats.

After rounding the Cape and laying her mines in the shipping lane off Cape Agulhas, Africa's southernmost point, *Atlantis* entered the Indian Ocean on 10 May, her presence undetected by the Royal Navy. Allied shipping in the area was caught completely unawares and the raider sank five ships, totalling 34,000 tons gross, in as many weeks. Encouraged by this early success, *Korvettenkapitän* Rogge searched around for more of the same. On 9 September, when the *Athelking* was sighted, he immediately increased speed to 17 knots, and altered course to intercept.

Rogge's change of course and speed was hidden from the British tanker by a passing rain squall, so by the time Captain

Tomkins of the *Athelking* became aware of her intentions less than 5 miles separated the two ships and the raider's guns were in plain sight. Tomkins sent his 4-inch gun's crew to their action stations, hoisted his colours, altered course to put the stranger astern, and asked the engine room for maximum revolutions. As the tanker began to pick up speed, he ordered his wireless operator to transmit the QQQ signal.

In response, Rogge hauled down his bogus Norwegian ensign and hoisted the German swastika in its place. When it was reported to him that the *Athelking*'s radio was alerting the world to her plight, he ordered his gunners to open fire. The range was close and the *Atlantis*'s initial broadside should have stopped the fleeing tanker in her tracks, but as the German gunners fired the *Athelking* suddenly sheered over to starboard and the carefully aimed shells went wide. At that critical moment, *Atlantis*'s electric steering gear chose to malfunction. Rogge sent his engineers running aft to the steering flat and the German ship was soon back on course, but she had lost the initiative.

The *Athelking* continued to run away and the two ships swapped shell for shell in a running fight that lasted most of the morning. It was a hopelessly one-sided contest, with a single ageing 4-inch manned by merchant seamen, pitted against the German's six 5.9s and a 3-inch, admittedly even more ancient, but in the hands of trained gunners.

There could be only one conclusion. Hit time and again, the tanker was soon ablaze from end to end. However, throughout the exchange the *Athelking*'s wireless operator had remained at his key sending the QQQ signal, and his courage had not been entirely in vain. His calls for help were picked up by the British steamer *Benarty*, westbound some 300 miles to the north-east, and her operator relayed the QQQ to all stations. Unfortunately, the few Allied warships stationed in the Indian Ocean at the time were concentrated in the north and there was little likelihood of help reaching the *Athelking*. Furthermore, in relaying the tanker's signal, the *Benarty* also gave away her own position, which was duly passed to *Korvettenkapitän* Rogge on the bridge of the *Atlantis*.

The *Benarty*, a 5,800-ton coal burner owned by Ben Line Steamers of Leith, was on passage from Rangoon to Liverpool with a cargo of lead, zinc and wolfram. As she was armed only with the usual

4-inch, and already sagging under the weight of her cargo, it was unlikely the *Benarty* would be able to offer *Athelking* much assistance. However her master, Captain Watt, was duty bound to answer the tanker's call for help and he altered course for the position given. In doing so, he sealed the fate of his own ship.

D/F bearings taken of the *Benarty* gave Rogge her approximate position, which *Atlantis* reached at about 1000 hrs the following day. Casting around, she eventually sighted a ship on her port quarter at about 18 miles, and the Heinkel spotter plane was flown off to investigate. If she was the *Benarty*, as Rogge suspected, the pilot was instructed to first bring down her wireless aerial with his trailing hook, then to use bombs and machine-guns to bring her to a halt. The aerial attack was a complete failure, however, and the Heinkel returned to land alongside the *Atlantis* and report to Rogge. Meanwhile the *Benarty* had reversed course and was fast disappearing over the horizon. Rogge left the aircraft in the water and took after the British ship at 17 knots.

Ageing she may have been, but the *Benarty*'s engine had been well maintained and was still capable of producing 13 knots, so the chase was prolonged and it was nearly sunset before *Atlantis*'s guns were within range. At 3,400 yards Rogge opened fire, first putting a shot across the *Benarty*'s bow and then, when she still refused to stop, straddling her with salvoes that started a number of fires on deck. Captain Watt, with one man already dead and others injured, fearful of more casualties, stopped and surrendered his ship. The *Benarty* was then boarded and sunk with scuttling charges, Watt and his crew being taken prisoner.

The *Benarty* was not the only Ben Line ship in the Indian Ocean at the time. Ben Line, founded in the days of sail to carry marble from Italy, had over the intervening years built up a substantial trade with the Far East with a fleet of fast, superior cargo liners. Based in Leith, the company was a family-run business, being largely owned by the Thomson family from Leith and the Mitchell family from Alloa. The ships were mainly Scottish manned, with Hong Kong Chinese firemen in the engine room. The 5,872-ton *Benavon* was no exception. Built on the Clyde in 1930, she was commanded by 44-year-old Captain Andrew Thomson and carried a crew of forty-eight. She was armed with a 4-inch and a 12-pounder, both mounted at her stern.

With a cargo of hemp, jute and rubber on board, the *Benavon* had sailed from Penang on 31 August, and when she heard the *Benarty*'s QQQ signals she had already passed her position and was some 540 miles to the south-west. Captain Thomson had been warned before sailing from Penang that a German raider was at large in the Indian Ocean, so he assumed this was the one involved with the *Benarty*. To reverse course and go to the aid of the other ship would have been pointless, so Thomson carried on, seemingly safe in the knowledge that the enemy was behind him. Unknown to Thomson, however, the *Atlantis* was not the only threat he had to contend with in these otherwise tranquil waters.

Following in the wake of the others, the commerce raider *Pinguin*, under the command of *Fregattenkapitän* Ernst-Felix Krüder, had sailed from Kiel in mid-June with orders to operate in the Indian Ocean. Requisitioned by the German Navy while still building in the winter of 1939/40, she was a half-sister to the *Atlantis* and originally named *Kandelfels*. When converted, she was in all aspects identical to her half-sister, similarly armed and manned. She also carried mines with orders to lay them off Cape Agulhas to replace the minefield laid by the *Atlantis* which, due to the premature explosion of one mine, had been discovered and swept by the Royal Navy.

Escorted through the Skagerrak and out into the North Sea, the *Pinguin* sailed around the north of Scotland, successfully evaded British naval patrols and entered the Atlantic through the Denmark Strait on 1 July. Adopting the disguise of the Greek cargo ship *Kassos*, she set course to the south, but it was not until a full month later, on 31 July, that she met her first victim, the British tramp *Domingo de Larrinaga*.

Owned by the Larrinaga Steamship Company of Liverpool, the 5,358-ton *Domingo de Larrinaga* was 300 miles north-west of Ascension Island, and homeward with a cargo of grain from Bahia Blanca, when sighted. *Pinguin* altered course to intercept, but her disguise did not fool Captain William Chalmers, commanding the *Domingo de Larrinaga*. He at once turned away and began sending the QQQ signal. Krüder attempted to jam the British ship's distress signals, but without success. He then opened fire with his 3-inch bow chaser and, when this failed to stop her, used his main armament to set her on fire. Eight of the *Domingo de*

Larrinaga's crew of thirty-six were killed before Captain Chalmers lowered his colours and surrendered. Scuttling charges laid aboard the British tramp failed to explode and Krüder had to resort to a torpedo to sink her.

The *Pinguin*'s opening sortie had not been impressive, but lessons were learned. Rounding the Cape on 20 August, the raider laid her mines off Cape Agulhas without difficulty, then went on into the Indian Ocean, where she sank another three ships, one British and two Norwegian, this time with comparative ease.

It was now September and *Fregattenkapitän* Krüder decided it was time for a change of identity. Moving south to a more remote location he set his crew to work with paint brushes, and the *Kassos* became another of Wilhelmsen's Far East traders, the *Trafalgar*. This transformation was completed by 10 September, when the *Pinguin* returned to the shipping lane south of Madagascar to await her next victim.

At 0645 hrs on the morning of 12 September 1940, with the sun just lifting from the horizon and the prospect of another fine day ahead, the *Benavon* was 330 miles due east of Cape St. Mary, the southernmost point of Madagascar, confidently steering a west-south-westerly course at 12 knots. Ahead lay Durban and a twenty-four hour break to take on bunkers and, of equal priority, to stock up with fresh provisions for the voyage home. On her bridge, Chief Officer James Cameron was in the chartroom plotting his morning star sights on the chart, Cadet Graham Spiers was in the wing keeping a lookout and Able Seaman Magnus Slater was at the wheel. God was in his heaven, and all was well with the *Benavon*.

A few minutes after 0700 hrs, as the smell of frying bacon wafted up from the galley heralding the end of the watch and breakfast, Cadet Spiers was searching the horizon to port with his binoculars, when he caught sight of a ship hull-up broad on the bow. He was unable to identify her, but it was clear that she was approaching the *Benavon* at speed. He called the Chief Officer from the chartroom. Cameron joined Spiers in the wing and ran his binoculars over her. By now her ensign was visible, the familiar blue cross on red of Norway. As she drew closer it seemed clear that she was one of Wilhelmsen's, a familiar sight in these waters. Satisfied that the stranger was friendly, Cameron relaxed, but as she appeared to be steering to pass ahead of the *Benavon* he delayed his return to the chartroom. Minutes later, it became obvious that the two ships were on a collision course.

Under the International Collision Regulations, the Norwegian, being on the *Benavon*'s port side, was the 'giving way ship', yet she showed no sign of doing so. In fact, she was by now less than 5 miles off and appeared to be intent on running the British ship down. In broad daylight, with unlimited visibility, this was clearly ludicrous. Cameron reached for the whistle lanyard and gave her a long warning blast. Then he sent Spiers to call Captain Thomson to the bridge.

By the time Thomson reached the bridge the approaching ship was little more than a mile away and still coming straight for the *Benavon*. Grasping the severity of the situation, Thomson ordered the helm hard to starboard and gave a double ring on the engine room telegraph. The *Benavon* surged forward and sheered away from the other ship just in time to avoid a collision.

It was now obvious to Captain Thomson that this was no chance encounter in an otherwise empty ocean and he steadied the *Benavon* on course with her stern to the stranger, intending to put as much distance between the two ships as possible as quickly as possible. As he did so, the *Pinguin* hoisted her true colours and broke out the two-letter flag signal 'SN' at her yardarm. Two flags, one simple unambiguous message 'YOU SHOULD STOP IMMEDIATELY. DO NOT SCUTTLE. DO NOT LOWER BOATS. DO NOT USE THE WIRELESS. IF YOU DISOBEY I SHALL OPEN FIRE ON YOU'.

Krüder followed up this challenge with a shot from his bow-chaser that whistled across the *Benavon*'s bridge. Ignoring the threat, Thomson replied by ringing for more speed and ordering his 4-inch gun's crew to their action stations. In his cabin abaft the *Benavon*'s funnel, Chief Engineer R. C. Porteous was still asleep, but his sleep was light and he was soon wide awake as the engine revolutions increased and the propeller raised its beat as the ship turned under full helm. He was out of his bunk in seconds and, throwing on a few clothes, tumbled out onto the deck. As he emerged into the daylight the *Pinguin*'s warning shell hit the water close by, throwing up a tall column of water. The raider was no more than 500 yards off on the port beam, with all her starboard guns exposed and trained on the *Benavon*.

Porteous ran for the bridge, flew up the access ladder and burst into the wheelhouse. There he found the pyjama-clad Captain Thomson in full control of the situation. Thompson's first words were, 'Morning, Chief. Get below and give me everything you've got!' Not one to mince his words either, Porteous replied 'Right!' and slid back down the ladder to the deck. Reaching the engine room minutes later, he spun the main steam valve wide open, and the flashing pistons of the *Benavon*'s triple-expansion engine threshed even faster. The chase was on.

Right aft, on the *Benavon*'s poop deck, Second Officer James Robertson, the ship's Gunnery Officer, had assembled his motley gun's crew around the 4-inch and was lining the gun up on the attacker. The activity was observed from the *Pinguin*, and *Fregattenkapitän* Krüder gave the order for all guns to open fire.

What was bound to be a one-sided duel almost came to a premature end when the first shell from the *Benavon*'s 4-inch – probably the first fired from the gun in anger since Jutland – ricocheted off the water and scored a hit on the *Pinguin*'s hull in way of her after cargo hatch. A lucky shot it may have been, but the British shell penetrated the raider's plates, glanced off a ventilator shaft and landed in the Stokers' Mess. This could well have been the death knell of the *Pinguin*, as in the compartment immediately adjacent to the mess were 300 sea mines destined to be laid off Australian ports.

Fortunately for the *Pinguin* and her crew, the *Benavon*'s inexperienced gunners had omitted to fuse the shell before loading and it failed to explode. Unaware of this, Bootsmann Streil, who was passing through the mess at the time, whipped off his cap and used it to carry the still smoking missile to the ship's side, hurling it back out through the jagged entry hole.

Completely unaware of how close he and his ship had come to oblivion, *Fregattenkapitän* Krüder was becoming increasingly annoyed by what he viewed as the futile resistance being put up by the British merchantman. The *Benavon*'s gunners had now got the range and her 4-inch shells, fused or not, were landing too close to the *Pinguin* for comfort. Krüder ordered his 5.9s to up their rate of fire, altering course as necessary to bring all guns to bear. Meanwhile, the British ship, having worked up to a speed that was threatening to pop every rivet in her Clyde-built hull, was zig-zagging wildly as she ran for the horizon, her amateur gunners lobbing shells at her pursuer with gay abandon. However, this could never be more than a last-ditch show of defiance. No further hits were scored on the German raider. On the other hand, the *Pinguin's* navy-trained gunners were doing no better. Her six 5.9s fired eight full salvoes, a total of forty-eight shells, before they landed a hit on the fleeing merchantman.

Unfortunately for the *Benavon*, this long overdue strike was a killer blow. The German shell hit the ready-use ammunition locker on her poop causing a massive explosion. When the smoke and flames cleared, the *Benavon's* 4-inch gun and its gallant crew had disappeared. Now unopposed, the *Pinguin's* gunners began the systematic destruction of their target. The *Benavon's* mainmast was first to go, toppling like a falling tree and bringing her main wireless aerial down with it. Radio Officer Charles Clarke, who throughout the gun battle had stuck to his key sending out distress signals, switched over to the emergency aerial only to find that that too had been brought down. The *Benavon's* last link with the outside world had been cut.

Minutes later, the funnel took a hit and that fell too. Without it, the *Benavon's* boiler furnaces were starved of air, the fires died, and she began to lose way through the water. She had put up a good fight and now would have been the time for Ernst Krüder to have shown some humanity by ordering his gunners to cease fire. It was not to be. The unexpected resistance put up by the British ship had aroused his anger and he was determined to punish her. Shell after shell continued to rain down on her, mercilessly wrecking her accommodation, smashing her upperworks, setting her on fire from stem to stern. Her four lifeboats were reduced to smouldering matchwood, the dead and wounded lay everywhere.

Much as he hated the thought of it, it was now clear to Captain Thomson that he must abandon his ship before more lives were lost. Reluctantly, he gave the order to launch the liferafts. This was the last order he would ever give, for at that point a full salvo from *Pinguin's* 5.9s scored a direct hit on the *Benavon's* bridge, wiping out almost everyone on it. Captain Andrew Thomson died with his face to the enemy, as did Chief Officer James Cameron, Third Officer John Milne and First Radio Officer Charles Clarke, while the helmsman, Magnus Slater, was seriously injured. Only then, when this once-proud cargo liner was leaderless and battered beyond all recognition, did the German gunners cease fire.

Chief Engineer Porteous, driven out of his engine room by smoke and flame, reached the deck to find himself, as the senior surviving officer, in sole command of what was left of the *Benavon*. With this came the responsibility of saving all those on board left alive. The options open to him were not great. The lifeboats had been lost in the fight. That left only the liferafts.

At that time most British ships carried, in addition to their lifeboats, four large wooden rafts, which were normally stowed on ramps at the foot of each mast, two each side. The rafts were double-ended and double-sided, capable of floating either way up. The flotation was provided by kapok-filled tanks and the rafts were equipped with mast and sails, paddles, distress flares and a supply of food and water. They were heavy, cumbersome craft, but a means of survival for desperate men.

It was found that two of the *Benavon's* liferafts had gone the way of her lifeboats, wrecked by gunfire, and of the remaining two, one was inaccessible due to the fires raging around it. Porteous launched the other raft with the assistance of Second Engineer Crawford and Boatswain Ollason, and twenty-four survivors, many of them wounded, followed it over the side. The wounded were put aboard the raft, while the others held onto the sides. As the raft drifted slowly away from the burning ship's side, Third Engineer Johnson died of his wounds and was eased over the side to make way for another.

The lone raft, almost hidden beneath the bodies clinging to it, was a pitiful sight, but *Fregattenkapitän* Krüder, still smarting from the insulting way the British liner had ignored his calls for surrender, was in no hurry to be merciful. He waited a full hour before sending a boat to their rescue. The stopped and drifting *Benavon* was first boarded and searched, five more survivors, three of them injured, being found. Only when the boarding party was on its way back to the *Pinguin* were the twenty-three survivors clinging to the liferaft picked up. In all, twenty-eight British prisoners were taken back to the raider. Of these, three died aboard the *Pinguin*, one of whom was the *Benavon* helmsman, Magnus Slater.

The unequal battle between the *Pinguin* and the *Benavon* had lasted for over an hour, during which the raider fired fifty-nine shells from her 5.9s before the British ship succumbed. Pounded to the waterline, the *Benavon* was finally left to burn herself out under a funereal pall of oily black smoke from the rubber in her cargo.

Before leaving the scene of his victory, *Fregattenkapitän* Krüder had the decency to bury with full military honours the three British seamen who had died aboard his ship. The twenty-five remaining survivors, seven British and eighteen Chinese, joined the other prisoners of war incarcerated in the raider's holds.

CHAPTER SIX

Retribution

His duty to the dead discharged *Fregattenkapitän* Krüder set course to the east, trawling the busy sea lane between Australia and the Cape. Before proceeding further with the voyage he was looking for a loaded tanker, suitable to sail in company with the *Pinguin*, refuelling her as necessary. At about 0400 hrs on the morning of 27 August, the tanker *British Commander* was sighted and challenged. She attempted to escape, but after a short chase was stopped by *Pinguin's* guns. When it was discovered that she was on a ballast passage with nothing more than sea water in her tanks, she was sent to the bottom with a torpedo. Her crew joined the other prisoners already in *Pinguin's* hold.

Three weeks later on 16 September, the Norwegian tanker *Nordvard* was sighted. She appeared to be deep-loaded and Krüder saw her as a possible supply tanker for the *Pinguin*, but on being stopped and boarded it was discovered the *Norwegian* was carrying a cargo of bulk grain in her tanks. Grain of any sort was at a premium in blockaded Germany and, rather than sink the tanker, Krüder put a prize crew on board and dispatched her to Bordeaux.

The *Pinguin* now sailed north-eastwards to straddle the Australia/India route and on 7 October came across yet another Norwegian tanker, the *Storstad*. This time Krüder had really struck oil – the *Storstad* was loaded with 12,000 tons of diesel and 500 tons of heavy fuel oil. The two ships sailed in company for Australia where, between 28 October and 7 November, strategic minefields were successfully laid off Melbourne, Sydney, Newcastle and Hobart.

Krüder's orders were to then search to the south and west for potential victims. On 17 November the *Storstad*, acting as scout for the *Pinguin*, sighted British India Line's 7,920-ton *Nowshera* homeward bound from Australia with a cargo of zinc ore, wheat and wool. *Pinguin* was informed and she raced in to send the *Nowshera* to the bottom. A similar fate attended Shaw, Savill and

Albion's 8,011-ton *Maimoa,* carrying frozen meat, butter, eggs and grain, which was sunk three days later.

Another twenty-four hours elapsed and Port Line's 8,739-ton *Port Brisbane* sailed into the arms of this successful pair. She was also deep-laden with meat and general supplies for British ports. Being armed with two 6-inch guns, she attempted to fight and run, but *Pinguin's* first salvo was deadly accurate, wrecking her wireless room, killing the radio officer on watch, and setting fire to her bridge. She was eventually sunk by torpedo.

A quiet period followed. Then on 30 November, another link in the Australia/Britain food chain sailed into the German net. She was the *Port Brisbane's* sister-ship, *Port Wellington,* sagging under a full load of lead ingots, frozen lamb, cheese and butter, with bales of wool stowed four high on deck. Commanded by Captain Emrys Thomas, the *Port Wellington* carried a crew of eighty, which included three Royal Australian Navy gunners, who were on board to lead the ship's guns' crews manning her armament of two 6-inch guns, one 12-pounder and six machine guns. Also on board were ten passengers, a Salvation Army party of three men and seven women, returning home after escorting British school children being evacuated to Australia.

Fourth Officer Edward Gilham described the encounter:

> We left Adelaide on the 20th November, 1940, and proceeded independently for Durban. We intercepted information about raiders operating in the vicinity, and during 24th November we intercepted messages sent by the *Maimoa* and *Port Brisbane* stating that they were being attacked by a raider. Unfortunately, both these ships sent out RRR (I am being attacked by an enemy surface warship) instead of QQQ (I am being attacked by an enemy merchant raider), which gave us the impression that there was something too big to tackle; a warship or cruiser. There were three courses open to us; we could reduce speed and steer south, continue on the course laid down by the Australian Admiralty, or return to Fremantle to rebunker. The Captain chose the second course, so we continued as routed.
>
> Nothing of further interest occurred until 1050 on the 30th November, when a tanker was sighted about

7 miles away. The Master decided at the time that it was just an ordinary tanker going to Australia, but we learned later that it was the Norwegian tanker *Storstad*, which had been captured by a German raider some time previously. The raider had put a prize crew on board, and was using her as a kind of lookout ship.

We continued on our westerly course, steaming at 12 knots, when at 2350 on the 30th November, 1940, in position 32° 10′ S 75° E (approx), we sighted a vessel about 2 points on the starboard quarter. The weather was fine, very dark, but visibility was good; there was a calm sea with moderate swell and light airs.

Being the junior of the *Port Wellington*'s navigating officers, Gilham would not normally have been in sole charge of the watch on the bridge. However, with the weather being fine, and there being very few other ships around, the opportunity had been seized to make a start on the backlog of maintenance on deck that had been piling up. Accordingly, Chief Officer William Bailey, who would normally have been keeping the 4 to 8 watch on the bridge, was spending his time on deck supervising the work. This involved all the other officers moving up a watch, and Fourth Officer Gilham, under the watchful eye of Captain Thomas, was temporarily in charge of the 8 to 12.

Proud of his new-found responsibility, Gilham paced the starboard wing of the bridge with the measured tread of a seasoned watch keeper. At the helm, Quartermaster Jim Waggot hummed quietly to himself and held the ship on course with economical movements of the wheel. Both men were counting the dying moments of the watch. At a quarter to midnight, Waggot leaned forward and struck the bridge bell once, signalling to the stand-by man that it was time to call the next watch. Gilham stopped his pacing and raised his binoculars to scan the horizon ahead. Nothing. He then turned to look aft and was astonished to see the dark outline of a ship close astern, not more than a quarter of a mile off and stealthily overtaking the *Port Wellington*.

Young Edward Gilham may have been short on experience, but he was not lacking in common sense and it was obvious to him that the other ship was up to no good. He altered course to put the stranger astern and called Captain Thomas to the bridge. His report continues:

> Without any warning, the raider turned her search-light on us and opened fire with one of her 5.9" guns at a range of about ¼ mile. I learned later that she fired 9 rounds, but I only heard 7 explosions, so two of the shells must have missed. The first shell wrecked the wireless cabin, killing the Senior Wireless Operator. The first two were oil shells, which immediately set fire to the wire-less room, Wireless Officer's cabin and the Smokeroom, which were all in one block, and by the time we aban-doned ship the fire had spread to the Engineers' accom-modation. The third, which was an H.E. shell, went through the funnel and exploded; the Master, who was on his way to the bridge at the time, was severely injured by splinters from it, and two days later died from his injuries aboard the raider. The other shells destroyed the passenger accommodation, the starboard 6" gun com-pletely disappeared and one of the gunners reported that the 12 pdr gun was also destroyed. One shell went into the ladies' bathroom and exploded in the wine locker. After firing about 9 rounds, the raider ceased fire, but continued to keep her searchlight on us.

As he lay on the bridge deck bleeding profusely, both his legs torn to shreds by flying shrapnel, Captain Emrys Thomas made one last defiant effort to save his ship. Handing over com-mand of the *Port Wellington* to Chief Officer William Bailey, he instructed him to ignore the enemy's shells and to continue to run away at all possible speed. Shortly afterwards, he lapsed into unconsciousness.

Bailey, thinking more logically than the injured captain, real-ized that the *Port Wellington*, with most of her main armament out of action and having a top speed of only 14 knots, had no hope of escaping. Accordingly, he stopped the ship and prepared to abandon her. Quartermaster Jim Waggot, who was at the helm at the time, described what happened next:

> Illumination provided by the flames erupting from the burning ship turned night into almost daylight. It was

then ascertained that it had only been possible to launch two of the ship's boats, the two on the port side being badly damaged by shellfire. On making a roll call it was found that the two boats collectively contained 80 crew members, six Australian Navy gunners, and eight passengers, ninety-four in total, the Chief Radio Officer being the only crew member to have lost his life. There were several of the crew suffering from injuries and limb fractures.

Captain Thomas was in a critical condition, having been nursed by the female passengers during the action and then lowered into a boat. It was almost impossible to provide medical attention for him in the cramped boat. The boats were taking water owing to the buoyancy tanks being damaged during the action. It was fairly obvious that they were not going to be capable of a long voyage with a large number of survivors.

The boats were within hailing distance of each other, and a discussion was taking place among the senior officers regarding the course to steer which would take us towards land, or better still, a shipping lane, when the sound of approaching motor launches was heard. They were manned by German Navy personnel armed with machine-guns, who in faultless English instructed us to row towards the German raider, where their Captain it was said wished to speak to us.

The nearest land being the island of Mauritius, about a thousand miles to the north-west, the survivors had reconciled themselves to a long and perilous voyage, but at least, assuming they survived, freedom would await them there. It was with mixed feelings therefore that they greeted the raider's boats when they came alongside. They were first ordered at gunpoint to row back to their ship, which, with Chief Officer Bailey as guide, the Germans boarded. The burning ship was thoroughly searched, scuttling charges were laid in her engine room, and her range finder, a rare addition to any ship's armament, was dismantled and lowered into one of the launches. The boats then went back to the *Pinguin*, where the survivors were taken aboard. Sadly, despite excellent medical attention in the *Pinguin*'s hospital, Captain Emrys Thomas did not survive the day. He was buried with full naval honours next day with some of the *Port Wellington*'s crew in attendance.

Fourth Officer Gilham takes up the story again:

> The name of the raider was the *Penguin* [*sic*], and in the prison accommodation I found the crews of thirteen other ships. She carried eight 5.9" guns, which were concealed by flaps on the ship's side, and an aircraft was kept in No.2 hold for scouting purposes. There was a collapsible house on the poop concealing a gun, whilst on the foc'sle head she carried some kind of submarine listening device which was supposed to be effective for about 60 miles. She also had a dummy funnel, which could be quickly rigged to make her into a two-funnelled ship, and she was fitted with depth charges and torpedo tubes.
>
> Altogether, there were 360 prisoners aboard the raider. Conditions were as good as could be expected, and on the whole the food was fairly plentiful. Three times each day we were allowed on deck for an hour's exercise, and during one of these airings smoke was sighted on the horizon. All the crew of the raider immediately became very excited: the Bo'sun of the vessel, who was in charge of the prisoners, was very friendly towards us, so I asked him what was happening. He replied that a British ship had been sighted, but when I asked him why the raider was not chasing it, he said it was only one of Smith's ships from Cardiff, and was not worth bothering about, especially as the raider was already overcrowded. He added, 'I cannot remember the name of the ship, but she is a small tramp and was at Adelaide with you.' I learned later that the Germans also knew the date the *Port Wellington* had left Adelaide, also what repairs were carried out in Australia, and with what guns she was fitted.

Edward Gilham must have been a shrewd young officer, for he also noted that there was a growing air of disillusionment in the lower ranks of the *Pinguin*'s crew. The main reason for this appeared to be that since leaving Germany, two weeks prior to the outbreak of war, their ship had already been at sea for fourteen months without so much as a sight of the land. On the other hand, in that time the raider had sunk or captured eleven

Allied merchant ships, amounting to 74,974 tons gross – no mean achievement. In spite of this success, the Germans were bored and, without a friend in these waters, not a little homesick.

Krüder had by this time had become concerned with the number of prisoners he had on board, fearing they might interfere with future operations. He signalled the *Storstad* to make a rendezvous, and seven days after the *Port Wellington* was scuttled the two German ships met up again. With a commendable show of magnanimity, Krüder offered his prisoners the choice of either transferring to the *Storstad*, which would then attempt to return to Europe, or remaining on board the *Pinguin*. Without hesitation all 360, presumably in the hope of better conditions, accepted to transfer to the supply tanker. Once they were aboard, the *Storstad* set sail for Bordeaux. Fourth Officer Gilham recorded:

Approximately 280 ratings were lodged in the fore hold, while 80 officers were battened down in a storeroom under the foc'sle head, which had two small openings, both boarded up, the only exit being through a small fore peak hatch, which was locked every night. We were issued either with a hammock or mattress, and one blanket, which I thought was very inadequate for a voyage round the north of Iceland. The food supplies were a disgrace; there was never enough to go round, consequently we were extremely hungry all the time. The guards were armed with hand grenades, revolvers, rifles, in fact anything they could get hold of. The conditions on board the Storstad were absolutely foul, the vessel was entirely unsuitable for carrying prisoners.

I do not know the exact course taken, but sometime in January (1941), after rounding the Cape, the STORSTAD contacted the ADMIRAL SCHEER, the Raider 'VIR', a smaller vessel which looked like a fruit ship and the DIXIE, a sister ship of the ALTMARK. During the next four days the STORSTAD re-fuelled these three ships, and food supplies were passed to us from the ADMIRAL SCHEER. All the food was from the Argentine, being part of the cargo of the s.s. DUQUESA. This ship had apparently been towed for some thousands of miles by the DIXIE and used as a store ship, with a prize crew on board. Our main diet from that day onwards was eggs. We were given about five every day, with bread and occasionally a slice of Libby's corned beef.

Escorted by two Italian submarines, which had mysteriously appeared at the rendezvous, the *Storstad* reached Bordeaux on 4 February 1941. There, the British prisoners were taken ashore, eventually ending up in a prison camp near Bremen, where they were to spend the rest of the war. The camp was a definite improvement on the cramped existence they had endured on board the *Storstad*, but conditions were still far from good. Edward Gilham had this to say:

> At this camp we found some men who had been taken prisoner a fortnight after the outbreak of war; they told me that before Dunkirk conditions were extremely bad, but they had gradually improved. After the fall of Tunis, and during the last eight months of my stay, the organisation of the camp was well nigh perfect. The food, however, remained very poor, and but for the Red Cross parcels, which we regularly received, I do not think I should be alive today. We were each given about 4 slices of hard black bread a day, and our main diet consisted of mangelwurzels. Potatoes, carrots etc. were very scarce, especially during the summer months, and during the months of June, July, August, September we practically lived on barley soup, the ration being one bowl of soup per day, together with bread, a very small portion of margarine, which I heard was made from coal, one spoonful of jam, and one spoonful of sugar. This was hardly enough to keep body and soul together, and, as I have said, had it not been for the Red Cross parcels, a great number of the prisoners would have starved.

Relieved of his prisoners, *Fregattenkapitän* Krüder, meanwhile, was free to tackle what he considered would be the ultimate of *Pinguin's* first war patrol, a raid on the Norwegian whaling fleet, which was known to be working near South Georgia. The raider sailed south and west until, on 14 January 1941, the first of the whalers was sighted. Taken completely by surprise, the Norwegians offered no resistance and Krüder captured a supply ship, two factory ships, eleven whalers, along with 20,000 tons of whale oil, valued at more than four million US dollars, and 10,000 tons of fuel oil. And all this without a shot being fired. This was a major victory for the German Navy and will long be remembered as the finest achievement of any surface raider in either of the World Wars. *Pinguin* then returned to the Indian Ocean, where in the spring of 1941 she sank three more British ships loaded with cargoes from the East, including Clan Line's *Clan Buchanan*. This ship was to be her undoing.

The 7,266-ton *Clan Buchanan*, launched at Greenock in December 1937, was a twin-screw, 17-knot cargo liner sailing under the command of 57-year-old Captain Douglas Davenport-Jones, with a total crew of 121, of whom 23 were British officers, 96 were Indian ratings and 2 were gunners seconded from the Royal Navy. She was armed with a 4.7-inch gun, a 12-pounder, two Hotchkiss machine-guns and two PAC Rockets. Carrying a cargo of military stores from the USA to India, the *Clan Buchanan* had left from Durban on 19 April 1941. Sailing alone, she was about 700 miles north-east of the Seychelles, when at dawn on the 28th she was intercepted by the *Pinguin*. Chief Officer S. S. Davidson, who was on watch on the bridge at the time, wrote in his report to the Admiralty:

> I heard shells bursting on and around the ship. The sea at the time was slight with a slight swell, wind light airs and variable, weather was fine and clear, and visibility was very good; daylight was breaking. We were making 15 knots on course 067°. We had not heard or seen anything previously.
>
> I went over to the starboard side of the ship to see what was shelling us but all that I could see were gun flashes on the starboard quarter about 3–4 miles away. By this time the Captain had come on the bridge and I asked him about his Naval Books. The 4ᵗʰ Officer and I went to the side of the ship and threw overboard the confidential books, the Radio Officer did likewise with the wireless books, and the Captain threw overboard the two special Admiralty bags of mail. Everybody was up by this time.
>
> When the Captain appeared on the bridge I asked him for orders and he ordered me to go to the boats, which

were already swung out, and see that they were ready to be lowered.

I proceeded to the boat deck and cut the gripe lashings of the boats so that they were ready to be lowered, as the natives had become a little panicky. The raider continued shelling us with salvoes of three shells about every minute. I noticed that the boat deck was riddled with shrapnel and that with the excepton of No.3, all our boats had been damaged by shrapnel.

As I returned to the bridge a shell struck the bridge and I found the Captain was in communication with the raider by morse lamp. The raider put up a signal 'Cease using your wireless or we will continue shelling you.' We replied that our wireless was broken. After the first salvo from the raider, the 2nd Wireless Officer got away an S.O.S. message and immediately smashed his valves and set with an axe. The engines had stopped. The protection around the 4" gun had been hit and pieces blown down the skylight into the engine room, and the natives had panicked from the engine room and stokehold.

The raider ceased shelling us about 0525, after 10 minutes continuous firing, and sent her motor boat alongside our ship with a boarding party, consisting of Commander Waring (No.1) and six heavily armed ratings, who came on board and took charge of the bridge. They demanded the secret papers, which had already been dumped and were not forthcoming. By this time the Captain had ordered the boats into the water. No.1 boat had been damaged too badly to be lowered, but the other lifeboats were lowered and the crew were standing by the ship in three lifeboats. In the meantime, fire had broken out on the after part of our ship. I called out to the 2nd Engineer, who was in one of the boats, to come back to the ship, and with the help of the 3rd Officer, who came down from the bridge, and the German sailors, we put out this fire.

After looting anything movable, food, wines, tobacco, and any papers found in the cabins of the senior officers, the German boarding party returned to their ship with Captain Davenport-Jones and his entire crew of 120 (24 Europeans and 96 Indians) as prisoners of war. For much of the time, the prisoners were kept locked away below deck, with regular periods for exercise on deck. By pertinent questioning of his fellow prisoners and the guards, and keeping his eyes open when on deck, Chief Officer Davidson compiled the following inventory of the *Pinguin's* equipment:

> Whilst on deck I noticed that the ship's armament was a 4" gun at her bow, two small guns on either side of the deck at the forward part of the bridge which looked like 12-pounders; these guns were swivelled at the base and dropped into two boxes lying on deck to resemble deck cargo. On either side of No.2 shelter deck they had a 5.9" gun. I heard from other prisoners that they thought that torpedo tubes were forward of those guns on the same deck. On the after part of No.4 shelter deck there was a 5.9" gun on either side and another 5.9" gun on the poop. There were also listening posts amidships on either side of the main deck and one on the bridge; they use[d] to throw something over the side when listening, but although we craned our necks we could not discover what it was. The ship appeared to have a lot of small posts on her deck to chain back the sides of the vessel as they cleared for action. A swimming tank lay on the starboard after end of No.4 hatch. There were two collapsible steel sampson posts on her after part which could be lowered by hinges. On top of No.5 hatch there was a big case, which obviously contained a gun, as the case was hinged and we could see that it fell apart: it looked like a 12-pounder to me but I did not see it opened. From the crew of the EMPIRE LIGHT, who had also been captured by the raider, I learned that searchlights were hoisted up to the ship's cross trees as required. Her crow's nest on the foremast could be lowered when required. There was no mine protective gear on the bow of the raider.

After sinking the *Clan Buchanan*, the raider had moved north and west into the Arabian Sea searching for a suitable loaded oil tanker from which to replenish her tanks. On 7 May, the 3,663-ton *British Emperor* was sighted. Signalled to stop, the British tanker ran for the horizon with her wireless operator sending out frantic distress signals. She was eventually stopped and sunk by the *Pinguin*'s guns, but her calls for help were heard far and wide – even as far away as Germany it was said.

Davidson's account continues:

> At 1000 on the 8th May, prior to returning to our cell after exercise on deck, our Captain was again told about the prisoners being brought up to the main deck. On this day we gathered from the amount of activity around the decks that something unusual was happening. At lunch-time this became more obvious, as our famous soup had no salt in it, also the prison guard outside our cell was dressed in his best and had his lifebelt and gas mask handy. No exercise was allowed that afternoon and during the course of the afternoon various alarms were sounded throughout the ship and we heard Germans running to their action stations.

Davidson's fears were well founded. Early that morning, a look-out in *Pinguin*'s crow's nest had sighted a warship on the horizon to the north, which *Fregattenkapitän* Krüder at once concluded could only be British. In fact, the distress messages transmitted by the *Clan Buchanan* and the *British Emperor* had set the alarm bells ringing loud. The light cruisers HMNZS *Leander* and HMS *Hawkins*, the aircraft carrier HMS *Eagle* and the heavy cruiser HMS *Cornwall* had all put to sea and were carrying out an extensive search for the reported raider. It was the last-named heavy cruiser that had now been sighted on the *Pinguin*'s horizon.

Krüder, unwilling to pick a fight with such a superior opponent, altered course and steamed away to the south-west at full speed, but *Cornwall* followed, flying off her Walrus to investigate the stranger. The flying boat circled the *Pinguin*, challenging her to identify herself. The raider, which was flying the Norwegian ensign, identified herself as the motor vessel *Tamerlane*. The pilot of the Walrus was not satisfied with this and radioed back to *Cornwall*, where the list of merchant ships currently in that area was consulted. The *Tamerlane* was not on that list. The chase was on.

When the British cruiser was first sighted, Krüder was well aware that he would eventually be forced to fight or surrender, but at first he kept his guns hidden, running away and continuously sending RRR reports, as would any Allied merchantman when under threat. Using her superior speed, HMS *Cornwall* closed on the German raider, signalling her by lamp to 'Heave to, or I fire!' *Pinguin* ignored *Cornwall*'s signals and continued to run. A shot across her bows produced no result and this was followed up by two 250lb bombs dropped by one of the cruiser's aircraft. Still the *Pinguin* refused to stop and the chase went on. Finally, at 1714 hrs, with sunset approaching and the range down to 5 miles, *Pinguin* suddenly dropped her disguise, altered sharply to port to present her full broadside of 5.9s, and opened fire, her shells straddling her pursuer.

Now the infamous 'Murphy's Law' intervened. *Cornwall* was about to reply with the full weight of her 8-inch guns, when the electrical circuits of her turrets failed and they were unable to train on the target. The cruiser was forced to retire out of range of *Pinguin*'s guns to make repairs, and to make matters worse, as she dropped back all telephone communication between the bridge and the guns also failed.

By this time the distance between the two ships had narrowed considerably and *Pinguin*'s gunners registered a direct hit, cutting all communication between the cruiser's bridge and engine room and knocking out her steering gear. A second hit started a fire on *Cornwall*'s main deck. Fortunately, the cruiser's crew were able to make temporary repairs and the tables were soon turned. With a Walrus spotting the fall of their shells, *Cornwall*'s gunners were soon straddling the raider. *Pinguin*'s foremast was brought down and, accepting the inevitable, *Fregattenkapitän* Krüder ordered his men to set scuttling charges and to prepare to abandon ship.

Krüder's orders came too late. The British gunners had got the range and shell after shell crashed into the raider. Their next hit demolished the two 5.9s on the forecastle head, killing those manning them, while another salvo wiped out *Pinguin*'s bridge, killing *Fregattenkapitän* Krüder and his officers. From then on, the fight was completely one-sided, and ended with a direct hit on the German ship's No.5 hold, which contained 130 sea mines. The explosion that followed blew *Pinguin* apart. HMS *Cornwall* lowered her boats and began picking up survivors from the water, but only sixty German crew members and twenty-four Allied prisoners were still alive. Of the *Pinguin*, just a scattering of charred wreckage remained to mark her grave.

During the action, which lasted less than half an hour, *Pinguin's* gunners fired over 200 shells, while *Cornwall* replied with some 135. It was a brutal end to what had been a brilliant career lasting just a few days short of a year, during which the raider *Pinguin* had steamed over 59,000 miles and had sunk or captured 28 Allied merchantmen, totalling 136,642 tons gross. Four more ships were sunk by the mines *Pinguin* had laid off the Australian ports, bringing the total tonnage she accounted for in her brief career to 154,710 GRT.

CHAPTER SEVEN

The Merchant Gunner

In early December 1940, while the *Pinguin* was busy offloading her prisoners onto the supply ship *Storstad*, the latest addition to Germany's fleet of commerce raiders was preparing to sail from Kiel. She was the 8,736-ton *Kormoran*, built as the *Stiermark* for Hamburg-America Line's East Asia run. An 18-knot ship, she had been requisitioned by the German Navy within months of the outbreak of war and converted to an armed merchant raider with the usual concealed 5.9-inch guns, one 3-inch, plus two 1.5-inch cannons and a variety of small calibre machine-guns. All these arms, as might be expected, were left-overs from the 1914–18 war – at least one of the 5.9s had seen action at Jutland – but in the hands of highly-trained naval gunners, they were expected to be lethal enough for the work they would be called upon to do. Like her predecessors, the new raider was also equipped with six 21-inch torpedo tubes, and launching racks for the 390 naval mines she would carry were fitted at her stern. To aid her reconnaissance, the *Kormoran* would carry two Arado Ar 196 float planes.

Fully stored and fuelled, the *Kormoran*, manned by a crew of 400 naval personnel and commanded by 37-year-old *Korvettenkapitän* Theodor Detmers, sailed from Kiel on 3 December 1940. Her orders were first to operate in the Atlantic against unescorted Allied merchantmen, then to move into the Indian Ocean to seek out similar targets, before laying her mines in the approaches to selected Indian and Australian ports.

When the *Kormoran* broke out into the North Atlantic through the Denmark Strait, she found an ocean unusually devoid of shipping. The only vessels encountered were flying the Stars & Stripes of the USA. They were tempting targets, but as America had not yet entered the war, strictly off limits for Detmers. After two weeks of frustratedly trawling the empty wastes of the North Atlantic Detmers decided to move south, and within hours his decision was justified by the sighting of a Greek steamer, *Antonis*.

At the time Greece was also neutral, but when stopped and boarded the 3,729-ton *Antonis* was found to be carrying a cargo of Welsh coal and had some British machine guns on board. This was excuse enough for her to be sunk.

Continuing southwards, *Kormoran* came across the British tanker *British Union* sailing alone and unescorted: she followed the *Antonis* to the bottom. Eleven barren days followed, then on 29 January 1941, in mid-ocean, Blue Star Line's 11,900-ton refrigerated cargo liner *Afric Star,* homeward with a cargo of frozen meat and butter, was encountered and despatched with torpedoes.

Theodor Detmer's blood was now well and truly up and he took *Kormoran* in towards the Gulf of Guinea, where there was said to be shipping in plenty. This proved to be true as that night, within hours of entering the gulf, the *Eurylochus* steamed into his sights.

The 5,273-ton *Eurylochus,* owned by Alfred Holt's Blue Funnel Line, was a typical British cargo liner of her day, twenty-nine years old, but still capable of a good turn of speed, well-maintained and competently manned. She had served with distinction in the First World War and had spent the years between the wars in the Far East trade. Again under the wing of the Admiralty, she was now bound for Egypt with a cargo of military stores, calling first at Takoradi, on West Africa's Gold Coast, to land sixteen engineless bombers. These would then be engined by the RAF in the port and flown to North Africa, for use in operations against Rommel's Afrika Korps.

Under the command of Captain A. M. Caird, RNR, the *Eurylochus* carried a crew of 81, which consisted of 14 British officers, 63 Chinese ratings, 3 naval gunners and one merchant seaman/gunner. This last mentioned 'odd-man out' was Frank Laskier, later to become something of a media star. Born in the squalor of Liverpool's dockland in the same year as the *Eurylochus,* Frank Laskier ran away to sea when he was fifteen and spent the inter-war years drifting from ship to ship, often drinking too much, spending time in prison, and looking in other words the epitome of a British merchant seaman as seen through the eyes of many ashore. When war came in 1939, he took a round turn, trained as a seaman/gunner, and in 1940 was serving aboard the *Eurylochus.* He later became an unofficial radio

spokesman for the British merchant seaman at war. Describing
Frank Laskier, the journalist Douglas Reed had this to say:

> Here was a humble man without money or schooling.
> Yet he spoke the tongue that Shakespeare spoke. His
> voice was soft but inescapable. He knew Shakespeare,
> and could interweave Shakespeare's phrases with his
> story so that they sounded as if they were spun that very
> moment. When he spoke you could hear the waves thud
> and smash against the sides, feel the ship lurch and stag-
> ger as the torpedo struck, see the men, with strained faces
> and blowing hair, toiling to get the boats out. He minted
> his own phrases, too, and they came out shining gold.

Some three and a half hours after sinking the *Afric Star*, *Kormoran*
was 600 miles due west of Freetown and on a south-easterly
course. It was a fine warm night, with a calm sea and excellent
visibility. Under these conditions, the shadowy outline of the
Eurylochus was spotted by the raider's lookouts almost as soon
as she came over the horizon. Detmers ordered his men to their
action stations and altered course towards the unidentified ship
which, as she was not showing lights, he assumed to be Allied.

Fourth Officer Alec Sparks was in charge of the watch on the
bridge of the *Eurylochus*, Chief Officer MacGregor having gone
below for dinner:

> I was on watch at the time, and at about 1830 ship's time
> (2020 GMT) heard a loud explosion as from gunfire, and
> at the same time a star shell burst over the vessel. It was
> very dark and overcast at the time.
>
> I sounded the alarms for action stations and gave the
> stokehold and the engineers due warning.
>
> In a few seconds the Captain arrived on the bridge and
> commenced conning the ship, ordering me to my gun sta-
> tions, my position being on the gun's crew.
>
> The first explosion was immediately followed by gunfire.
>
> I would say that the first round from the enemy was at
> an opening range of about 4,000 yards.
>
> While I was on my way aft to man the gun the enemy
> succeeded in hitting the vessel – probably about his
> twelfth. The first hit disabled the steering gear and the

gun, causing one casualty, at the same time setting the magazine on fire. The Gunlayer instantly flooded the magazine.

Seaman/Gunner Frank Laskier described the action more vividly:

> One night – 800 miles from land – I was on watch on the (4-inch) gun. At half-past six it was pitch dark on a tropical night. Suddenly there was a shot and a bang, and into the air there shot an enormous great yellow flare. I turned round and made one wild dash for the gun, and as I got to the gun, suddenly a hell, an absolute holocaust of shells burst around us. They were firing on the starboard beam, complete broadsides, those six 11-inch guns and eight 5.9-inch guns. [Laskier was under the impression that their attacker was the pocket battleship *Admiral Scheer*, which only three months earlier had laid waste to the *Jervis Bay* convoy in this area.]
>
> Quick, up to the gun, open the breach, ram the shell, ram the charge home, close the oven door, stick the tube in, run to the trainer, train her round, quick, quick, and crash the shells are banging into us. Round she's trained, the lights are there, try to get on the searchlight, duck under the muzzle, put your range on, bring it down, bring it down; pull the trigger. Bang went old Mildred. It was heaven.
>
> Back aft, open up again, put the shell in, and then . . . . there was a crash like the opening of the Gates of Hell.
>
> I was thrown about six feet. I picked myself up and there was just no gun worth speaking of left. Up to my feet, round the poop, down the ladder, across the well-deck, stepping on a bloody gruel of men's bodies who had been smashed as they came out of the poop; up the ladder, along the upper-deck. God, where's the bridge? – There isn't any. . .

The above is a wonderful example of spontaneous descriptive writing by a man who was in the thick of the fight. Reading between the lines, it would appear that Laskier, who was on watch on the 4-inch gun platform when the *Kormoran* attacked, loaded, aimed and fired the gun single-handed. This was the action of a very brave man, who fails to mention that in this 'holocaust' he lost his right foot to an enemy shell.

Captain Caird later described the action in his official report:

> 6.32 p.m. Star shells, raider opened up without warning from 6,000 yards on the port quarter, took eight salvoes to get the range; the first hit put out the steering gear and gun which had not been fired, but the raider continued to fire salvo after salvo down to 3,000 yards, even after I had stopped the ship and signalled that I was abandoning, which was acknowledged by flashlight; a direct hit was scored on the bridge with the next salvo. A second raider came up to starboard and opened fire by searchlight. [There is no evidence that a second raider was present. In fact, it was later confirmed that the *Kormoran* was operating alone. The likely explanation is that the *Eurylochus* swung around when she stopped, bringing the raider onto her starboard side.] Machine-gun bullets were sprayed fore and aft, the bridge receiving good attention, and continued while we were trying to get away from the ship; two boats were shot to pieces, the other two got away but I fear a number of lives were lost. Launched two rafts from the poop when a salvo from 500 yards hit the port side amidships. The few of us still on board took to the water as the ship started to settle at 6.55; she sank at 7 p.m.

Chief Officer J. A. C. MacGregor added in his report:

> Wireless silence was maintained until after the first salvoes were fired. We signalled 'We are going to abandon ship', there was no response to this signal but the attack was concentrated on the lifeboats, while the rafts received a certain amount of attention from the machine-gunners.

Fourth Officer Sparks confirmed the surrender:

> Just previous to the hit on the bridge, the Captain had given the order to abandon ship, and I flashed with a torch from the bridge to the enemy that we were abandoning ship, which was acknowledged.

On receipt of the message he re-opened fire and hit EURYLOCHUS in way of No.2 hatch. He then closed further and machine-gunned us, but without effect.

Korvettenkapitän Detmers gave a rather different account of the action:

Once or twice it seemed to me that her stern fired at us, but then our gunners got her range with deadly accuracy. Within a few minutes the *Eurylochus* gave in, stopped her engine and ceased using her wireless. I then ordered the cease fire and switched on the searchlight. We stopped at a distance of about 1,000 yards from her and lowered the motor-boat with the usual boarding party. They went aboard, made a quick search of the ship and placed the explosive charges. After a while two life-boats came in sight and were ordered alongside. We got all the prisoners below, our motor-boat came away and after a while the charges exploded. While we were on the bridge watching the slowly sinking ship my wireless room reported that the wireless of the *Eurylochus* was in action again. I ordered the 2 cm anti-aircraft to open fire on the midships structure and after a few moments the wireless activity ceased. That was one more reason for sinking the *Eurylochus* quickly and getting away from the neighbourhood; I therefore ordered my Torpedo Officer to finish her off, and this he did. Just as the torpedo leapt out of its tube, something moved into our searchlight; it was one of the ship's boats. I immediately gave orders for a signal to be morsed 'Torpedo Away'. Unfortunately the time was too short for this to have effect, and the boat arrived at the side of the *Eurylochus* at the same time as our torpedo. There was a terrific explosion as the tor-pedo hit the *Eurylochus* amidships. Our searchlight lit up again immediately, but there was no sign of the boat or anyone in the water near the *Eurylochus*, which was now settling down rapidly. We sailed around in a circle in the hope of picking up survivors, but we found nothing.

Fourth Officer Alec Sparks later gave his version of the evacuation of his ship:

I first went to No.1 boat to lower it down but found the coils of the falls had been cut away by the Chinese crew. I then gave orders to drop the boat, letting both falls go together. The boat fortunately landed upright in the water and was instantly filled with Chinese – some jumping into the water, others sliding down the falls. The Second Officer went down the ladder and took charge of this boat.

I then went to No.3 boat but found it unfit for lowering owing to damage by gunfire.

I then went to No.4 boat station but found that the boat had disappeared, apparently having been taken away by the Chinese.

I reported the condition of the boats to the Captain and he ordered me to get the rafts away. In the meantime we tried dragging the wounded to a position of cover.

Intermittent shellfire from the enemy was kept up throughout.

Whilst on the poop, just after getting the starboard raft away, a shell hit the vessel on the starboard side and travelled right through leaving a big hole on the port side and throwing the hatches up from No.5 hatch.

Shortly after this another shell hit the vessel by No.4 hatch.

We then got the port raft away and took it along midships on the painter.

The well deck on the port side was now only about four feet above sea level and we dropped the wounded over the side and picked the two worst wounded up from the raft, another not requiring assistance.

The Captain and the Chief Engineer then left the vessel and joined us on the raft; and when we left the vessel there were seventeen people aboard the port raft.

We paddled well clear of the vessel, keeping the calcium flare under water. After paddling for about half an hour we made contact with the other raft, but the Chinese aboard her were very reluctant to close. The Fourth Engineer and the Chief Cook paddled over themselves and we then just lay quiet for a while, and we lashed the two rafts together.

Just before this the EURYLOCHUS had gone down stern first at about 1930 (2130 G.M.T.).

As the ship was going down the enemy kept a searchlight on the name and on the ship as if trying to see what the cargo was.

We lay quiet for a while until the enemy stopped using his searchlights, and as the swell was increasing we decided to separate the rafts. Whilst doing this the other raft overturned and all the Chinese were thrown into the water and the two Europeans were hauled onto our raft. We then counted how many were in each raft and four Europeans transferred across to the Chinese raft to balance the numbers.

The enemy had now departed and we drifted and kept the raft head on to the sea, keeping the paddles going. At daylight we saw the other raft still around and there was also an empty raft about a mile away from us. The Captain decided to paddle over to this empty raft in order that we might transfer some of the officers and also to get the food which, on our own raft was under water, owing to being over-loaded.

At about 1330 we were about 50 yards from this empty raft when we sighted the smoke of a steamer on the horizon. This steamer approached our position and when about two miles off heaved-to. We tried to attract her attention by waving improvised flags, blowing hand whistles and shouting. This apparently attracted the steamer's attention for he altered course towards us and we saw that she had everything ready for receiving us on board.

We eventually paddled alongside the Spanish MONTE TEIDE and the survivors from the two rafts were taken on board.

The 6,193-ton *Monte Teide*, a Spanish-flag passenger/cargo vessel, commanded by Captain P. Munecas, was on passage to Buenos Aires, but after taking the *Eurylochus* survivors on board from the raft, interrupted her passage to search for more of their kind. She found only wreckage. No lifeboats, no rafts, no bodies.

Later that day, the *Monte Teide* made a rendezvous with the British armed merchant cruiser HMS *Bulolo*, which was responding to *Eurylochus*'s SOS calls. The survivors were then transferred to the AMC, with the exception of Captain Caird and Chief Engineer Creech, who stayed with the Spanish ship to look after the Chinese ratings, who were unhappy at being carried on to Buenos Aires.

In the short and bloody gunfight between the *Kormoran* and the *Eurylochus*, ten of the British ship's crew were killed and several others were wounded. It was later learned that *Kormoran* had picked up four British and thirty-nine Chinese from the British ship's boats and from the water. None the worse for the encounter, *Kormoran* had then headed north to keep a rendezvous with the supply ship *Nordmark* off the Cape Verde Islands. There the raider took on supplies and handed over the 170 prisoners she carried, including those from the *Eurylochus*. All these men would eventually end up in a prisoner-of-war camp in Germany. *Kormoran* then moved south again, to meet up with her fellow raider *Pinguin* in order to collect some desperately needed white metal to reline her worn engine bearings.

On 15 March, *Kormoran* met *U-124* with the intention of supplying her with torpedoes, provisions and engine spares, but the weather was too bad for the transfer to be made. Both raider and U-boat then headed south, where the sea was calmer. In a remote part of the South Atlantic they met the cruiser *Admiral Scheer*, and the three vessels spent a few congenial days together exchanging supplies, before returning to the war.

Kormoran went east, then south, and at dawn on 9 April, near the Equator and some 300 miles east of St. Paul's Rocks, a large merchant ship was reported coming up astern. Called to the bridge, Kapitän Detmers at first thought the overtaking ship might be a British armed merchant cruiser, but on closer examination decided she was just a fast cargo carrier sailing alone. He slowed down to allow her to overtake.

Detmers' assumption had been correct. The overtaking ship was in fact a British gauntlet runner, T & J Harrison's 8,022-ton *Craftsman*, on passage from Rosyth to the Middle East with military supplies, calling first at Cape Town to land an anti-submarine net. The net, a huge steel mesh suspended from buoys 5 feet in diameter, was to be used for the defence of Cape Town harbour, and took up much of the space in the *Craftsman*'s cargo holds.

Commanded by 61-year-old Captain W. E. Halloway, the *Craftsman* was a 14½-knot ship, and quickly drew abeam of the

Kormoran, passing on her port side about 3 miles off. At that point, the raider increased speed, exposed her guns, and signalled 'STOP OR I FIRE!' In response, Halloway ordered his wireless operator to start transmitting the QQQ (I am being attacked by an enemy merchant raider) signal, and sent his gunners to man the stern gun. *Kormoran's* wireless room intercepted and jammed the *Craftsman's* calls for help and the raider opened up with her 5.9s, scoring immediate hits on the British ship.

The *Craftsman* increased speed and attempted to escape, at the same time returning *Kormoran's* fire with her 4-inch, but the exchange was short and bloody. In the space of ten minutes the British ship was reduced to a burning wreck, her Captain blinded by flying sand from sandbags protecting her bridge and five of her crew lying dead. She had no choice but to stop and surrender. A boarding party from the raider laid scuttling charges in the *Craftsman's* engine room but, kept afloat by the buoys of the anti-submarine net in her hold, she refused to sink. Eventually, Detmers had to resort to torpedoing her. Forty-six survivors were taken on board the *Kormoran* as prisoners.

Kormoran now rounded the Cape and entered the Indian Ocean, where she continued her random attacks on Allied shipping. She sank several merchantmen, but her happy hunting days were rapidly drawing to a close. A large number of warships were now searching for her, but by adopting various disguises she managed to escape discovery until mid-November when, masquerading as the Dutch steamer *Straat Malakka,* she was sighted off the north-west coast of Australia by the light cruiser HMAS *Sydney.*

On 19 November, the *Sydney,* commanded by Captain Joseph Burnett, RAN, was some 80 miles off the coast of Western Australia, in the region of Caernavon, searching for the *Kormoran,* which was reported to be in the area. At around 1600 hrs, lookouts in the cruiser sighted an unidentified merchant ship steaming north at about 11 knots. Burnett altered course to intercept, whereupon the stranger immediately presented her stern and ran away at full speed. The *Kormoran* had been caught napping.

Sydney gave chase, signalling by lamp and flag for the ship to identify herself. In reply, the *Kormoran* hoisted the *Straat Malakka's* signal letters and began transmitting the QQQ signal, indicating she was under attack. This was standard procedure, as recommended by the Admiralty, except that Detmers had used the wrong code. His operator should have sent RRR, which signifies an attack by an enemy warship, whereas QQQ indicates that the attacker is a merchant raider.

Captain Burnett was immediately suspicious and challenged the *Kormoran* again, demanding that she reply with her secret call sign, as per the British Merchant Navy code. This Detmers could not do and, accepting that the game was up, he ordered the German ensign to be hoisted and the gun shutters raised.

What happened then is a matter for conjecture; but both ships sank, HMAS *Sydney* with the loss of all hands, while those who survived from the *Kormoran* were reluctant to talk. It has been suggested that a Japanese submarine intervened and torpedoed the *Sydney*, but this has never been substantiated. What seems probable, from the scant evidence available, is that Captain Burnett allowed the *Kormoran* to get too close – some say within 1,000 yards – and that Detmers opened fire with every trainable gun, at the same time emptying his torpedo tubes at the cruiser. HMAS *Sydney* was taken completely by surprise and simply overwhelmed, but not before she hit the *Kormoran* with a full salvo from her 6-inch guns, setting her on fire. The fire eventually reached the raider's magazine, or the hold where her mines were stowed, and she blew up and sank.

There were no survivors from the Australian cruiser; all 645 men on board died. It was a sad end to the career of Australia's best-loved warship, and she is remembered to this day. As for the *Kormoran*, 318 of her total complement of 398 managed to abandon ship before she blew up, and were saved. She had a relatively successful career over ten months and across two oceans, resulting in the loss of six Allied merchantmen, totalling nearly 70,000 tons gross – she can at least claim to have gone out in a blaze of glory.

CHAPTER EIGHT

A Challenge to the Big Guns

Norway, with its deep fjords fronting the North Atlantic, offered an ideal sanctuary for German warships and had for some time been a part of Hitler's grand plan for the conquest of Europe. This was known to British Intelligence and it came as no surprise when, on a dark, storm-swept morning in April 1940, German troops swarmed ashore in the approaches to Narvik. The hand of war had fallen on the as yet uncommitted Norwegian peninsula.

On that same morning, some 150 miles to the south-west of Narvik, off the Lofoten Islands, ships of the Kriegsmarine covering the invasion were hove-to in the teeth of a fierce gale, battered by mountainous grey seas and lashed by squalls of hail and sleet. Commanded by Vice Admiral Günther Lütjens, the German force consisted of the battlecruisers *Scharnhorst* and *Gneisenau* and an escort of ten destroyers. In the extreme weather prevailing, the destroyers, hard pressed to just remain afloat, could be discounted, but it was considered that the two battlecruisers, each mounting nine 11-inch and twelve 6-inch guns, would be quite capable of dealing with any attempt by the British to interfere with the landings. Then, out of the darkness to the west came Admiral Sir William Whitworth with the battlecruiser HMS *Renown* and nine fleet destroyers of the Royal Navy.

The battle that followed lasted just ninety minutes and was largely inconclusive, more damage being inflicted on both sides by the heavy seas than by gunfire. The big ships hurled shell after shell at each other but were rolling and pitching so violently that accurate aiming was impossible. Hits were scored by both sides, but none was of any real account. In the end, British firepower prevailed. In that short hour and a half, *Renown*, mounting six 15-inch and twenty 4.5-inch guns, fired a total of 230 rounds from her big guns and 1,065 rounds from her secondary armament. The fight was finally decided by the weather, breaking seas knocking out electrical circuits to the gun turrets of *Scharnhorst* and *Gneisenau* and forcing them to withdraw to the west. *Renown*, equally battered by the ferocious seas, was unable to give chase.

While the British and German battlecruisers fought themselves to a standstill off the Lofotens, German troops had been landing on the beaches of nearby Denmark. The tiny Danish army could offer only a token resistance and when the Luftwaffe threatened to raze the capital, Copenhagen, to the ground, it was all over. The Danish government had no other option but to surrender. When the sun rose on that morning of Tuesday, 9 April 1940, Denmark was in German hands.

News that his homeland had fallen under the Nazi jackboot reached Captain Anton Knudsen in the Indian Ocean, as noon sights were being taken on the bridge of his command, the 1,831-ton *Chilean Reefer*. Bound for New Zealand to load a cargo of frozen lamb, the *Chilean Reefer* was then enjoying weather that contrasted sharply with that prevailing some 6,000 miles away off the Lofoten Islands. Running before a barely perceptible north-easterly breeze, on a sea that was mirror-calm, her progress was marked by the slap-slap of a small school of porpoises that cavorted in her foaming bow-wave. Overhead, the sky was a faultless Indian Ocean blue, unsullied by even a wisp of cloud. Idyllic is the word that comes to mind.

Built by Nakskov Skibsvaerft in Denmark in 1936, the *Chilean Reefer* was powered by a 6-cylinder B & W diesel engine, which gave her a service speed of 14 knots, and was refrigerated in all four cargo holds. She carried a crew of thirty-nine, composed of Danish officers and Chinese ratings. Her owners, J. Lauritzen of Copenhagen, had begun business as a timber yard in 1884, moving into shipping four years later. Starting with one sailing ship, the *Frederikke Sophie*, they progressed into steamers and by the outbreak of the Second World War had accquired a substantial fleet of forty-seven vessels, eight of which were small refrigerated cargo carriers like the *Chilean Reefer*.

On that serene day in the Indian Ocean, where peace reigned, Captain Anton Knudsen had suddenly found himself facing a major dilemma; should he ignore the news from Denmark and carry on to New Zealand, thereby risking his ship being seized by the British Navy, or should he make for the nearest neutral port to seek refuge while he contacted his owners for orders? After some agonized deliberation, Knudsen settled for the latter and set course for Pandang, on the southern coast of Dutch-controlled Sumatra.

His decision was made too late, for within hours the *Chilean Reefer* was intercepted by a British warship and taken into Penang, on the west coast of Malaya. From there she was moved under escort to Singapore, where she was handed over to the British Ministry of War Transport, who in turn placed her under the management of Alfred Holt's Blue Funnel Line. She then proceeded to Cape Town, where her Danish crew were given the option of continuing to sail in her under the British flag, or being put ashore in South Africa. Captain Knudsen and all his officers, with the exception of Second Engineer Jacobsen, opted to go ashore; the Chinese ratings agreed to stay with the ship. Captain Thomas Bell, of the Blue Funnel Line, now took command and with the aid of a passage crew sailed the ship to London.

On 16 March 1940, the *Chilean Reefer*, fresh out of dry-dock and painted grey, left the River Tyne in ballast, bound west across the Atlantic. Captain Bell was still in command, but he now had with him a full team of eighteen British Blue Funnel officers, in addition to twelve Danes and six Chinese from her original crew. There was one other addition, a British naval gunlayer, who had the unenviable task of training up volunteers from the crew to man the ship's guns.

Third Officer Graham Sibly remembers:

> We took the ship to the Tyne for arming and alterations and apart from the museum piece of a 4-inch, we got a couple of Lewis guns, a P.A.C. of evil memory, a few rifles and a fog buoy. Thus we went to war. There was no cabin for the 3rd Mate so they made one for me out of the Master's entry lobby, and very nice it was, too, except that it had a thwartship bunk.
>
> From the Tyne we went to Methil and Loch Ewe for a convoy, thence to Montreal, where we loaded a full cargo of bacon. Well below our marks, we battled our way home in Western North Atlantic weather in a slow convoy, losing some seven ships to the U-boats on the way. After discharging at London, we anchored at Southend, waiting to join an East Coast convoy, and while we were there we witnessed the horrific sight of a Norwegian

tanker, inbound fully loaded with spirit, activate a magnetic mine and burst into flame fore and aft in the vicinity
of No.4 Sea Reach Buoy. All hands were lost, except one
Deck Boy, despite the efforts of an RN destroyer which
raced up from astern at full speed through the flames
to try to save at least some of the crew, but to no avail.
As the destroyer came out of the fire her ensign, signal
halyards and paintwork were on fire.

From Southend we went to Methil and Loch Ewe,
in convoy to about 25° W, and then on our own to
St. Johns, New Brunswick, for another cargo of bacon.

Graham Sibly left the *Chilean Reefer* when she returned to British
waters, and after a brief spell of well-earned leave, joined the
British tanker *Ajax*, sailing in five convoys for the relief of the
besieged island of Malta.

Meanwhile the German battlecruisers *Scharnhorst* and *Gneisenau*,
their work in the Norwegian campaign done, had made a number of sorties into the North Atlantic to attack Allied convoys,
with moderate success. In January 1941, after repairs to heavy
weather damage, they were ready to go out again. Their next mission, codenamed Operation BERLIN, involved the two capital
ships breaking out into the North Atlantic through the Denmark
Strait as before, thence to wreak havoc amongst Allied convoys
using the northerly route. This was at a time when the British
and Canadian escort forces were particularly stretched and convoys were being escorted only in the area where U-boats were
known to be active, which was largely in the western approaches
to the British Isles. Elsewhere they sailed unescorted or, at best,
accompanied by a single armed merchant cruiser.

The German High Command, in planning Operation BERLIN,
had anticipated another glorious success for the battlecruisers, but
in doing so they failed to take into account the notorious North
Atlantic weather. The winter and early spring of 1941 proved to
be one long succession of destructive storms that turned the great
ocean into a howling nightmare. The *Scharnhorst* and *Gneisenau*,
hunting within shell-shot of each other, once again found themselves being battered by hurricane-force winds and mountainous
seas and, more often than not, hove-to to avoid serious damage.
For some unexplained reason *Scharnhorst* was able ride out the

weather without significant damage, but *Gneisenau* suffered so badly that the operation was abandoned and both ships returned to port.

Essential repairs to the *Gneisenau* were carried out in Kiel and by 22 January the raiders were back at sea. They were spotted in the Skagerrak by Allied agents, who alerted London, and units of the Home Fleet were deployed to bar their passage between Iceland and the Faroes. The ambush failed when the British ships were detected at long range by radar and the German battlecruisers were able to take cover in rain squalls and enter the Atlantic unseen. A rendezvous was made south of Cape Farewell with the supply tanker *Schlettstadt* on 6 February and, having refuelled, *Scharnhorst* and *Gneisenau* began to prowl the convoy lanes again. They saw nothing until sunrise on the 8th, when a large eastbound convoy crested the horizon and steamed towards their loaded guns.

HX 106 was a convoy of forty-one loaded merchantmen bound for Liverpool. It had sailed from Halifax nine days earlier with a substantial escort of eleven warships. On passage, these escorts had been detached one by one for other duties until, in midocean, only the battleship HMS *Ramillies* remained. Although she was a relic of the First World War and hard-pressed to make 21 knots, *Ramillies* was armed with eight 15-inch and fourteen 6-inch guns. With this firepower the Admiralty considered her quite capable of warding off any attack until the convoy was met by escort destroyers in the Western Approaches.

The presence of this ageing battleship with HX 106 proved to be deterrent enough. Although *Scharnhorst* and *Gneisenau* were both superior ships, each mounting nine modern 11-inch and twelve 5.9-inch guns and being at least 10 knots faster than the *Ramillies*, the mere sight of the British battleship was sufficient to persuade Admiral Lütjens to hold back. He declined to attack the convoy and withdrew his ships to the north.

The German battlecruisers, having turned down the invitation to cross swords with the Royal Navy, continued to patrol the North Atlantic for another two weeks without sighting a single Allied ship, merchant or naval. It was not until 22 February that their efforts were finally rewarded by the appearance of a ragged collection of Allied merchantmen recently dispersed from convoy OB 285. Although these ships were considered to be clear of the U-boat danger area, they had remained huddled together – seeking protection in numbers, perhaps? When the two huge German warships swept down on them with guns blazing, the unescorted merchantmen scattered and ran in all directions. Four were sent to the bottom, three by the *Gneisenau* and one by the *Scharnhorst*.

Encouraged by the ease with which 26,000 tons of Allied shipping had been dispatched, Admiral Lütjens decided to move south and east to the Cape–Gibraltar route, where on 8 March the northbound convoy SL 67 was encountered.

Unfortunately for Lütjens, SL 67, consisting of fifty-four loaded Allied ships, was under very heavy escort, being accompanied by the battleship *Malaya*, the aircraft carrier *Ark Royal*, a Colony-class cruiser, two destroyers, a corvette and an armed merchant cruiser. Reluctant to exchange shots with such a powerful force, Lütjens again withdrew his ships.

Once out of sight, the German admiral contacted two U-boats known to be in the area, passing on the composition of SL 67 and its current position. The boats in question, *U-124*, commanded by *Kapitänleutnant* Georg-Wilhelm Schulz, and *U-105* with *Kapitänleutnant* Georg Schewe commanding, joined forces off the Cape Verde Islands and at dawn on the 8th moved in to attack the convoy.

Schewe, in *U-105*, was first to strike, torpedoing and sinking the 5,229-ton British steamer *Harmodius*, bringing the convoy's escort down on him like a pack of snarling dogs as a result. Schewe was forced to run deep and withdraw, but a diversion had been created that allowed *U-124* to attack undetected. In the space of just twenty minutes Georg-Wilhelm Schulz had sent another four British ships to the bottom with their cargoes. That morning SL 67, despite its heavy escort, lost a total of 20,514 tons of shipping to the two U-boats.

Scharnhorst and *Gneisenau* had meanwhile returned to mid-Atlantic, where twenty-four hours later they ran into another recently dispersed westbound convoy. OB 294, consisting of forty-two merchantmen, mostly in ballast, had sailed from Loch Ewe on 6 March, escorted by four destroyers and three Flower-class corvettes. As was the custom at the time, the escorting ships left the convoy in 20° W, and the merchantmen continued unescorted to their various destinations on the other side of the

Atlantic. All the ships being of similar speed they had continued westwards together in a loose formation, and on 16 March were 500 miles west of the Azores.

The German battlecruisers caught sight of this untidy gaggle of ships at about 0130 hrs on the morning of 16 March and immediately attacked. Caught completely unawares, the Allied ships scattered and ran. *Scharnhorst* and *Gneisenau* gave chase with their big guns blazing and it was all over by first light. When the guns fell silent and the smoke of battle cleared, thirteen merchantmen lay on the bottom of the ocean, a total of 61,781 tons of valuable shipping lost to the Allied cause.

Only one of the ships under attack succeeded in alerting the outside world to the fate of the dispersed convoy OB 294. She was the British tanker *Simnia*, owned by the Anglo-Saxon Petroleum Company of London. The *Simnia* was sailing in ballast from Stanlow to Aruba, and was the first ship of the convoy to be sighted by lookouts aboard the *Gneisenau*, which immediately closed in at full speed, opening rapid fire with her 5.9s. Five hits were scored on the tanker in quick succession and with three of his crew already dead the *Simnia*'s master, Captain James Anderson, accepted that resistance would only lead to more casualties. He stopped his ship and hauled down his flag. With her surviving crew members prisoners aboard the *Gneisenau*, the *Simnia* was sunk by gunfire.

While she was under attack, the *Simnia*'s wireless operator had sent out a series of RRR signals, but no help was at hand. The warning transmission was, however, picked up by the *Chilean Reefer* which was then only 50 miles to the east of OB 294. She was crossing the Atlantic alone, bound for Halifax, Nova Scotia. On receipt of the RRR, Captain Bell made a wide alteration of course away from the danger, increased speed, and took precautions in anticipation of an attack. The 4-inch gun was manned, extra lookouts posted, and the lifeboats were cleared away. The time was then 1600 hrs, and as the cover of darkness was then only two hours away Bell had high hopes of slipping past the danger unseen.

With the pistons of her 6-cylinder B & W diesel flashing, the *Chilean Reefer* surged forward, reaching for the safety of the night. Her normal service speed was 14 knots, but she was soon up to 16. As an extra precaution, knowing that any attacker would first try to bring down his wireless aerial, Bell had an emergency aerial rigged to the funnel. He could do no more.

As predicted, darkness closed in at around 1800 hrs, and with no moon and a heavily overcast sky the darkness was complete. There seemed no way that the *Chilean Reefer* could be seen, unless the enemy had radar. Unfortunately for the British ship, he did. Both *Scharnhorst* and *Gneisenau* were equipped with Seetakt, a relatively primitive form of radar with a range of up to 14 miles, depending on the prevailing weather. Seetakt had a fixed forward-facing aerial, so that only targets right ahead or close on either bow could be picked up, and often the echo was poor, as in this case, just a vague blip on the cathode ray tube.

Gneisenau, running down the unidentified echo on her radar screen, suddenly emerged out of the darkness on the *Chilean Reefer*'s port bow – so suddenly that the British ship's lookouts failed to sight her until it was almost too late to take avoiding action. Fortunately, Captain Bell was on the bridge and he reacted instinctively, putting the helm hard over to starboard and ringing for full emergency speed. The engine room was equally alert and Second Engineer Jacobsen, who had the watch, immediately spun open the control valve to its full extent. The *Chilean Reefer* leaned heavily as she came round in a tight turn to put the German raider astern. In the radio room abaft the bridge of the fleeing ship the duty operator, 18-year-old Third Radio Officer Crew, was well briefed and, without waiting to consult the bridge, he began hammering out the pre-arranged RRR message. As this plaintive cry for help went out over the ether, the *Gneisenau*'s shells were already straddling the *Chilean Reefer*.

Captain Bell ordered smoke floats to be launched to confuse the enemy's aim, and began to zig-zag violently in an effort to dodge the shells raining down on his ship, and for a while it almost seemed that escape was possible. Then the German battlecruiser's superior speed and immense firepower began to tell. As the range closed, more and more of the *Gneisenau*'s shells were finding their target. In an act of hopeless defiance, Bell ordered his 4-inch gun's crew to fire back.

The enemy ship was well within range of the *Chilean Reefer*'s ancient 4-inch and, under the direction of Second Officer Collett, the half-trained team of amateurs manning the gun gave of their best. And so the hopelessly one-sided fight went on, with Bell on the bridge, steering for the fall of the enemy's shot, while his seamen gunners lobbed shell after shell at the attacker. It is believed that one British shell did hit the *Gneisenau*, but no more.

So fierce was the resistance put up by the *Chilean Reefer* that the Germans suspected they were engaged with an armed merchant cruiser, and they redoubled their efforts to sink her. The *Gneisenau*'s 11-inch guns joined in the bombardment and a veritable hail of shells began to fall all around the British ship, yet she seemed to bear a charmed life as she zig-zagged wildly away. Then two German shells, possibly one of each calibre, found their mark, slamming into the *Chilean Reefer*'s accommodation and setting her on fire. Other strikes followed and the little ship was soon burning fiercely. Fearful that her lifeboats would be destroyed, leaving them with no means of escape, Captain Bell was forced to admit defeat. He stopped the ship and gave the order to take to the boats.

Although the *Chilean Reefer* was clearly hove-to and offering no further resistance, the *Gneisenau* gunners continued to pound her, causing some panic as the crew of the burning ship struggled to lower their boats. In the confusion the starboard boat was up-ended, spilling its occupants into the sea. The port boat was successfully launched and remained alongside while Captain Bell made one last search for anyone who might have been left behind.

By the time Bell boarded his boat, having found no more survivors, the wind and sea had risen considerably, but he insisted on searching for those lost from the starboard boat. While they were thus occupied, the *Gneisenau* had approached the *Chilean Reefer* and was shelling her at close range, as though determined to eliminate her altogether. It was later reported that the German battlecruiser used a total of eighty-two shells on her helpless victim and yet the British ship stubbornly refused to sink. Meanwhile Captain Bell had been ordered to bring his boat alongside the *Gneisenau,* but not wishing to be taken prisoner he ignored the order and carried on with his search for survivors. Eventually, the German raider gave up her pointless destruction and left the scene at full speed, almost swamping the lifeboat as she swept contemptuously past.

Nine of the *Chilean Reefer*'s crew had been killed in the action; three others would die later. Six men thrown into the sea from the capsized starboard lifeboat, including Second Officer Collett, were picked up by the *Gneisenau* and taken prisoner. The port lifeboat, heavily overloaded, partially swamped, and her tiller smashed by hasty departure of the German battlecruiser, had drifted off into the darkness. As the night wore on and the weather deteriorated the boat became unmanageable, but thanks to Captain Bell's foresight in rigging an emergency aerial, help was at hand. The *Chilean Reefer's* RRR had been heard by the battleship HMS *Rodney*, which along with other heavy units of the Royal Navy, was out searching for the commerce raiders, and she came racing to the scene of the battle. It is reported that she actually sighted the *Gneisenau* and flashed a challenge, which the German ship answered, claiming to be the British cruiser HMS *Emerald*. In the ensuing confusion, *Gneisenau* used her superior speed of 28 knots to escape into the night. *Rodney*, with a top speed of 20 knots, was unable to give chase.

After this near-miss with retribution, Operation BERLIN was abandoned, a decision that was due in no small way to the gallant fight put up by the diminutive merchantman *Chilean Reefer* and the RRR signal she was able to get away. However, Operation BERLIN must be considered a major victory for the two German ships; in this operation alone they sank a total of 107,704 tons of Allied shipping.

The victorious battlecruisers reached the Biscay port of Brest on 2 March, where *Gneisenau* went into dry dock to carry out long overdue maintenance. She was not allowed to rest easy in dock, being subjected to repeated raids by the RAF. On 6 April, the *Gneisenau* was out of drydock and at a lay-by berth in the harbour, when six Bristol Beaufort torpedo bombers of RAF Coastal Command attacked. The weather at the time was very bad and only one aircraft, piloted by Flying Officer Kenneth Campbell, got through to the target area. The story appears in an entry in the *London Gazette* dated 13 March 1942:

> Flying Officer Kenneth Campbell, 22 Squadron, Royal Air Force Volunteer Reserve.
>
> In recognition of most conspicuous bravery. This officer was the pilot of a Beaufort aircraft of Coastal Command which was detailed to attack an enemy battlecruiser in Brest harbour at first light on the morning of 6th April 1941. The aircraft did not return but it is known that a

torpedo attack was carried out with the utmost daring. The battlecruiser was secured alongside the wall on the north shore of the harbour, protected by a stone mole bending around it from the west. On rising ground behind the ship stood protective batteries of guns. Other batteries were clustered thickly round the two arms of land which encircle the outer harbour. In this outer harbour near the mole were moored three heavily armed anti-aircraft ships, guarding the battlecruiser. Even if an aircraft succeeded in penetrating these formidable defences, it would be almost impossible, after delivering a low-level attack, to avoid crashing into the rising ground beyond.

This was well known to Flying Officer Campbell who, despising the heavy odds, went cheerfully and resolutely to the task. He ran the gauntlet of the defences. Coming in at almost sea level, he passed the anti-aircraft ships at less than mast-height in the very mouths of their guns and skimming over the mole launched a torpedo at point-blank range.

The battlecruiser was severely damaged below the water-line and was obliged to return to the dock whence she had come only the day before. By pressing home his attack at close quarters in the face of withering fire on a course fraught with extreme peril, Flying Officer Campbell displayed valour of the highest order.

For his extreme gallantry in action Flying Officer Kenneth Campbell was posthumously awarded the Victoria Cross. He and his crew, Sergeant J. P. Scott RCAF, Sergeant W. C. Mulliss and Sergeant R. W. Hillman, were buried by the Germans with full military honours in Kerfautras Cemetery in Brest.

The sacrifice of the Beaufort and her crew was not in vain. Their torpedo blew a huge hole in the starboard side of the *Gneisenau*'s hull, causing serious flooding, and significant damage to her propeller shafts, while most of her electronic instruments were knocked out by the blast. She was returned to drydock, where the RAF found her and continued their attacks. In a heavy raid on 9 April, the battlecruiser was hit by four 500lb bombs which caused extensive damage and killed eighty-eight of her crew, wounding seventy-four others.

Gneisenau remained under repair in Brest until February 1942, when she was joined by the *Scharnhorst*, which had been moved to La Pallice during the bombing, in a suicide dash through the English Channel. Accompanied by the heavy cruiser *Prinz Eugen*, and escorted by motor torpedo boats and aircraft, the ships caught British forces napping. Steaming at 27 knots and hugging the French coast, they broke through the Dover Strait and entered the North Sea. The intention was for the two battle-cruisers to deploy to the Barents Sea to attack the Allied supply convoys to Russia.

Once clear of the Dover Strait, *Gneisenau*'s luck ran out again. Rounding the Terschelling Bank she ran onto a magnetic mine – ironically a German one – but escaped with only minor damage. Then, as she was about to enter the Kiel Canal she hit a submerged wreck and ended up back in drydock. There she again became a target for RAF bombers and, in a raid on the night of 26 February, a bomb penetrated her forward magazine causing a massive explosion which destroyed her forward turret and much of her bow section. Casualties were said to be 112 dead and 21 wounded.

Temporary repairs were made to her bow and the *Gneisenau* was moved to Gydinia in the Batltic, where it was hoped she would be safe from the RAF. There she remained until the end of the war. When Russian troops were advancing on the port in March 1945, rather than allow her to fall into Soviet hands, the *Gneisenau*'s crew took her out to the harbour entrance and sank her as a blockship. In September 1951 she was raised by the Polish authorities and at last sent to the breakers. Much of her steelwork was used in the rebuilding of the Polish merchant fleet.

CHAPTER NINE

Operation SUBSTANCE

Strategically placed in the Sicilian Narrows, commanding the mid-passage of the Mediterranean, Malta has long been the target of foreign invaders. Said to be first inhabited around 5,900 BC, it has since passed through the hands of the Phoenicians, the Romans, the Byzantines, the Arabs and the French, each occupier in turn using the island as the lynch pin to control the Mediterranean. The French occupation was brief, lasting for just two years, and brought to a close by the defeat of Napoleon's fleet at Aboukir Bay by Admiral Nelson in 1798. Nelson blockaded Malta for fourteen months, finally taking it for the British flag in September 1800. Malta was declared a British crown colony in 1813 and for the next 142 years was home to the British Mediterranean Fleet.

In the summer of 1941, some eighteen months into the Second World War, Malta lay astride the sea routes supplying Axis forces in Libya, ideally placed for British aircraft and submarines to harrass the enemy by attacking his convoys. This, in turn, made Malta a prime target for the 400 German and 200 Italian bombers and fighters based in Sicily and Sardinia. In support of the aircraft was the entire Italian Home Fleet, which could put to sea when required 5 battleships, 10 cruisers, 20 destroyers, 30 fast motor torpedo boats, and an unspecified number of submarines. While the Italian Navy was not known for its tenacity of attack, these were all modern, well-equipped ships, capable of creating havoc amongst slow, heavily laden merchantmen.

Malta, with only twenty or thirty RAF fighters to defend the island and its approaches, was under total siege, its cities in ruins from the incessant bombing, and was desperately short of anti-aircraft shells, aviation fuel, diesel oil and food. Time after time supply convoys had tried to get through from Gibraltar and Alexandria to raise the siege but had failed, and by April 1941 the day when surrender must be considered was drawing near. The situation had become so serious that the possibility of supplying the island by fast merchant ships, running the gauntlet unescorted and under false colours, was being considered. Churchill approved the scheme, and the 4,698-ton steamer *Parracombe* was selected to initiate the operation.

Built in 1928 at William Gray's yard in West Hartlepool, and owned by the Stanhope Shipping Company of London, the *Parracombe* had achieved considerable success in running supplies into Spanish republican ports during the Civil War of 1936–39. If any ship could get through to Malta with supplies, then she was the prime candidate. Commanded by Captain David Hook and manned by a crew of volunteers, she loaded a cargo of ammunition and war materials including twenty-one crated Hurricanes, and, disguised as a Spanish merchantman, sailed from Gibraltar on the night of 28/29 April 1941.

Once clear of Spanish waters, the *Parracombe* crossed to the Algerian side and changed her identity to that of a French freighter, hugging the coast as far as Cape Bon. It was proposed that once she reached the Cape she would then make a dash straight for Malta under cover of darkness, arriving within 50 miles of the island at dawn, where she would be met and escorted by the RAF. Codenamed Operation TEMPLE, the relief of Malta was under way.

Nothing further was heard of the *Parracombe* after she left Gibraltar, and it was assumed that she had either been sunk by Italian bombers or had run into an enemy minefield off Cape Bon. The latter assumption proved to be correct. The blockade runner had been warned of mines in the vicinity of Cape Bon and she had her paravanes streamed. One mine was cut adrift by a paravane and exploded at close range, but the damage done to the ship was negligible. Unfortunately, in sheering away from the explosion the *Parracombe* hit another mine with disastrous results. She sank shortly afterwards, taking her precious cargo with her. Thirty crew were lost with the ship, while seventeen survivors were taken prisoner by Vichy French forces. Second Radio Officer R. Proctor was amongst those saved. He later wrote:

> I struggled to get out on to the deck. Flames were shooting up from the engine room. On reaching the after deck tracer bullets and shells were shooting into the sky.

I decided it was time to take the 60-foot jump into the sea.

The ship was settling at an angle of about 50 degrees.

Following the loss of the *Parracombe* and the failure of Operation TEMPLE, four other attempts to run the blockade of Malta with single unescorted ships were attempted and failed. Success did not come until September 1941, when the 5,720-ton *Empire Guillemot* ran the gauntlet of enemy ships and aircraft, arriving in Valetta with a cargo of ammunition, fuel and fodder for the island's cattle. Sadly, the *Empire Guillemot* was sunk by Italian bombers on the return passage to Gibraltar. One of her crew was killed, while the rest were taken prisoner.

It so happened that Malta's hour of need coincided with Operation BARBAROSSA, Hitler's long-planned invasion of Soviet Russia. In order to support BARBAROSSA, it was found necessary to temporarily withdraw most of the Luftwaffe squadrons from the Mediterranean, leaving only the Italian bombers to maintain the siege of Malta. The code breakers of Bletchley Park learned of this situation and alerted the Admiralty in London. Encouraged by the success of the *Empire Guillemot*, the Admiralty decided to launch Operation SUBSTANCE.

Operation SUBSTANCE was primarily aimed at supplying Malta with sufficient food and ammunition to carry on the fight, but at the same time it was used to reinforce the island's garrison by delivering two infantry battalions, two anti-aircraft units, and a battery of thirty field guns. In order to achieve delivery, it was planned to run the gauntlet of the Mediterranean with six fast cargo liners and two troopships escorted by heavy units of the Royal Navy. The cargo liners selected for this mission were all British, namely Blue Funnel Line's *Deucalion*, Blue Star Line's *Melbourne Star* and *Sydney Star*, Ellerman Line's *City of Pretoria*, Federal Line's *Durham* and Port Line's *Port Chalmers*. Carrying the troops and their equipment would be the ex-French liner *Louis Pasteur* and the requisitioned passenger ferry *Leinster*.

The merchant ships loaded their cargoes at various British ports. Their crews were not told the destination of the supplies, but it was soon obvious to everyone concerned that something special was afoot. Fourth Engineer Stan Dodd, serving aboard the *Deucalion*, explained:

It was sensed that this was a special voyage because we were loading general food supplies and the *Deucalion* had limited but useful refrigeration cargo space, a lot of War Department equipment, loads of bully beef and endless 4 or 5 gallon drums of high octane aircraft fuel. The special voyage feel was confirmed when a contingent of soldiers (I think about 40 or 50) embarked. They had very basic accommodation. They carried all their own gear including sleeping bags and were made as comfortable as possible. I later learned that they were crack anti-aircraft gunners from the Cheshire Regiment.

The loaded ships were assembled in the North Channel in sight of the island of Oversay on the morning of 13 July. In the course of the day they were joined by the two troopships and an impressive naval escort consisting of the battleship HMS *Nelson*, the battlecruiser *Renown*, the light cruisers *Arethusa* and *Manchester*, the Dutch light cruiser *Heemskerk*, and the destroyers *Cossack*, *Lightning* and *Nestor*. The fast fleet minesweeper *Manxman* was in support. In overall command of the convoy, designated WS 9C, was Vice Admiral James Somerville, who flew his flag in HMS *Renown*. The convoy commodore was in the *Louis Pasteur*.

Once clear of the land, the convoy formed up into five columns abreast, with the battlecruiser *Renown* in the lead, the more vulnerable battleship *Nelson* in a sheltered position in the middle of the merchantmen, and the cruisers and destroyers guarding the flanks. A westerly course was set, the convoy steaming deep into the Atlantic until clear of the known hunting grounds of the U-boats. The ships then altered to the south and commenced their 1,200-mile passage to the Straits of Gibraltar. Only then did Admiral Somerville reveal the ultimate purpose of the convoy by sending a written message by destroyer to each individual merchant ship. The message read:

> For over twelve months Malta has resisted all attacks of the enemy. The gallantry displayed by the garrison and the people of Malta has aroused admiration throughout the world. To enable their defence to be continued, it is essential that your ships, with their valuable cargoes, should arrive safely in Grand Harbour. The Royal Navy will escort and assist you in this great mission, you on

your part can assist the Royal Navy by giving strict attention to the following points. Don't make smoke. Don't
show any lights at night. Keep good station. Don't strag-
gle. If your ship is damaged keep her going at the best
possible speed. Providing every officer and man realises
it is up to him to do his duty to the very best of his ability,
I feel sure we shall succeed. Remember that the watch-
word is 'the convoy must get through'.

Admiral Somerville's message may have been well intended, but
to many of those manning the merchant ships, who had been in
the thick of the fight for nearly three years and were well drilled
in convoy routine, it bordered on insult. Typically, they had been
kept in the dark about the actual destination of their cargoes,
but it really came as no surprise for it to be confirmed as Malta.
The 'galley wirelesses' had been buzzing with the word ever
since the first sling of cargo came over the rails.

What did impress those in the merchant ships was the unusual
strength of the convoy's escort. Radio Officer Robert Hamilton
serving in the *City of Pretoria* enthused, 'Our RN escort is amazing
– *Nelson*, *Renown*, at least six cruisers and many other warships
were in company.' DEMS gunner A. Cockburn, aboard the *Sydney
Star* remarked, 'I was comforted when the *Sydney Star* broke out
into the Atlantic with the rest of the convoy to find we were in
company with the *Ark Royal* and quite a number of heavy cruisers
and destroyers.'

The long run south was made in fine weather and, no doubt
mainly by virtue of its formidable naval escort and a convoy speed of 16 knots, WS 9C was not troubled by the enemy.
The powerful light on Cape St. Vincent, the south-western
extremity of Portugal, came abeam soon after dark on 19 July and
the convoy wheeled to port to approach the Straits of Gibraltar.
Not unexpectedly, for these waters are notorious for their poor
visibility, dense fog was encountered during the night, and the
early hours of the 20th were spent at a crawl as the ships felt
their way through the narrows.

By dint of careful navigation they reached anchorage in
Algeciras Bay soon after dawn, but there was little time for rest.
After only a few hours at anchor the convoy, redesignated as
Convoy GM 1, resumed its voyage. Now in overall command

was Rear Admiral Neville Syfret, who flew his flag in the cruiser *Edinburgh*. Captain David Macfarlane, in the *Melbourne Star*, was appointed convoy commodore.

An ominous indication of what might lay ahead, the convoy's escort had been reinforced by the aircraft carrier *Ark Royal*, with 24 Fairey Fulmar fighters and 30 Fairey Swordfish torpedo bombers on board, the light cruiser *Hermione* and 8 destroyers. Additionally, 8 Royal Navy submarines had been stationed along the route to Malta to counter any interference by the Italian Navy. With the object of creating a diversion, some seventy-two hours after GM 1 sailed from Gibraltar, six empty merchantmen would sail in Convoy MG 1 from Malta, bound west to Gibraltar. At the same time, units of the Royal Navy's Mediterranean Fleet operating out of Alexandria were to set up a continuous barrage of radio traffic, designed to clog up the airwaves and create even more confusion for the listening enemy.

Convoy GM 1 left Algeciras Bay after dark on the 20th, again in fog, which fortuitously served to hide the movement of the ships from the prying eyes of the many German agents on the Spanish shore. Unfortunately, the fog also put an end to the voyage of the small troopship *Leinster*, which ran aground in the Straits and was withdrawn from the operation.

Contrary to expectations, for the first forty-eight hours after sailing from Gibraltar the enemy made no move to interfere with the convoy, perhaps correctly anticipating a weakening of GM 1's escort. This in fact happened on the morning of the 23rd when the ships were entering the Sicilian Narrows, and within 250 miles of Malta. The battleship *Nelson*, the battlecruiser *Renown*, and the aircraft carrier *Ark Royal* were ordered to withdraw and return to Gibraltar. This left the protection of the merchant ships in the hands of the four cruisers, *Arethusa*, *Edinburgh*, *Hermione* and *Manchester*, plus the destroyers, the wisdom of which decision was open to question. However, in view of the vulnerability of the big ships to attack from the air they may have been considered to be more of a liability than an asset. Cape Bon was abeam to starboard when, at about 0920 hrs that morning, the first enemy planes made their approach from the north-west and the decision to withdraw the capital ships was put to the test.

It was a two-pronged attack by nine CANT Z 1007 high-level bombers and seven Savoia Marchetti SM 79 torpedo bombers of the Italian Air Force. The CANT 1007s, three-engined bombers with a crew of five and a bomb capacity of 2,560lbs, came in at about 5,000 feet, while the torpedo bombers, each carrying a single torpedo, approached simultaneously at wave-top height, thereby splitting the fierce barrage put up by the ships.

The Town-class cruiser *Manchester* was the first casualty. By skilful manoeuvring she had evaded the first three torpedoes aimed at her, but in doing so came very near to colliding with the *Port Chalmers* and, in avoiding hitting the cargo ship, ran straight into another torpedo. The explosion blew a 60ft hole in the cruiser's hull, causing serious flooding and disabling her port propellers. Twenty-six of her crew and twelve of the Army personnel she carried were killed. Partially crippled, *Manchester* carried on, but the most she was able to make was 9 knots and she was unable to keep up with the convoy. Eventually, she was ordered to return to Gibraltar escorted by the destroyer *Avon Vale*.

HMS *Fearless* was the next to be hit. The destroyer was torpedoed amidships, caught fire and had to be abandoned. Fourth Engineer Stan Dodd of the *Deucalion* was an eye-witness to the attack:

> We were all depressed watching her crew jumping over the side. They would no doubt be picked up as there was plenty of help around. Some Italian airmen had been shot down and baled out into rubber dinghies. They were mockingly trying to thumb a lift from us. After seeing the *Fearless* go down you can imagine how we were all feeling. One of the Cheshire Regiment soldiers standing alongside me had his rifle trained on the dinghy, but one of the officers walking past tapped him on the shoulder and said, 'We don't do that in the British Army.'

Fearless's sister destroyer HMS *Forester* was quick to come to her aid, but although she was able to pick up some survivors, thirty-five men were lost. *Fearless* was later sunk by gunfire from the other destroyers.

The Italian air attack did not go unchallenged. The carrier *Ark Royal*, returning to Gibraltar, was only just over the horizon, and four of her Fulmars came racing back to shoot down four of the enemy planes. The AA guns of the ships accounted for another three. Seven more Fulmars arrived on the scene and succeeded in foiling another attack by high-level bombers, but three of the British planes were shot down.

The Italian planes then flew away, but were back again before it was dark and made two more attempts to savage the convoy. They found the ships negotiating a mined area, steaming in two columns abreast, each column being led by a destroyer with her paravanes streamed. HMS *Firedrake*, leading the port column, was hit by a bomb and holed. With the destroyer *Eridge* escorting, she joined the procession of lame ducks heading back to Gibraltar. GM 1's escort was slowly but steadily being pared down. Fortunately, when darkness closed in the attacking planes lost contact with the convoy. The ships then made a diversion to the south, setting course to pass close to the island of Pantellaria. They were now within ten hours steaming of Malta and they raced through the night at 16 knots, leaving the flares dropped by the searching Italian bombers visible to the north. With luck, they would be in sight of their destination by morning.

The night that followed was long and tense, and towards dawn spirits were flagging when the roar of high-revving engines was heard approaching from the north. Those who had been here before knew that sound and made ready, helmets on and life jackets to hand as they closed up on the guns. Searchlights clicked on from the escorting cruisers and destroyers, and sweeping the darkness revealed a covey of eight fast Italian motor torpedo boats bearing down on the convoy with creaming bow-waves. These were the dreaded *Motoscafo Armato Silurante* of Mussolini's *Regia Marina*, 45-knot MTBs, powered by Isotta Fraschini engines and each armed with two 18-inch torpedoes and heavy machine guns. Stan Dodd wrote:

> We could hear the E-boats in the pitch dark roaring through the shipping lanes and we could hear the aircraft above. Frequently the destroyers exposed their search-lights and then let go with everything they had – it was all acrid smoke, brilliant blue and orange as the big guns were fired and then a few seconds of dark and quietness, until the next time. All this went on for quite a few hours.

To be more explicit, 'all this' meant the screaming roar of high-speed engines, the staccato hammer of machine guns, the thunder of the escorts' guns, the scything streams of tracer – and above it all the drone of aircraft engines as the Italian bombers, attracted by the sweeping searchlights, came to join in the fun.

On the bridge of the *Sydney Star* Captain Tom Horn watched in horror, mesmerised by the fiery streams of tracer reaching out for his ship. It was now the darkest hour before the dawn and he was unable to identify his attackers, but he had been here before and the roar of the Italian MTBs' engines was unmistakeable. He edged away in a new zig-zag pattern. As he did so, the confusion worsened when an unidentified merchantman on his starboard side opened up with her 4-inch and shells began to whistle over the *Sydney Star*'s bridge. Inevitably, one of these rogue shells slammed into her boat deck, demolishing one of her lifeboats. Then, amongst all this mayhem, Horn became aware of the sleek outline of an MTB some 50 yards off the starboard beam and running parallel to his ship. He ordered his gunners to open fire.

At that point the cruiser *Edinburgh*, which was close by, intervened, opening a devastating fire with her 4-inch guns and multiple pom-poms, literally blowing the fast Italian craft out of the water, but as the burning debris of one MTB fell apart, another came racing out of the darkness and launched a torpedo at the 11,000-ton *Sydney Star*.

The heavily laden ship was too big a target to miss. She was hit squarely amidships, in way of her No.3 hold, the exploding torpedo tearing a hole 30 feet by 20 feet in her hull. The cargo in the hold, much of which was aviation fuel, immediately caught fire and a great plume of flame soared skywards, only to be suddenly extinguished as the Mediterranean poured into the breached hull.

Horn rang the engines to stop and the *Sydney Star* slowed to a halt and lay drifting in the current, which was carrying her gradually towards the tall cliffs of Pantellaria, now less than 3 miles to starboard. Damage control parties were hard at work shoring up the watertight bulkheads of the breached hold, but they were unable to stop the sea seeping into No.2 hold; the *Sydney Star* was settling by the head.

The prospects looked bleak and, mindful of the troops he was carrying, Horn instructed his radio officer to send out a call for help. This was quickly answered by the Australian destroyer *Nestor*, which manoeuvred alongside and took off the 484 men of the 32nd Light AA Regiment and most of the *Sydney Star*'s crew. Horn and a small party of volunteers stayed with the ship and, after an inspection of the damage, decided that it might be possible to bring her into Malta.

The rescue operation had taken just fifty minutes and, with the *Nestor* escorting, the *Sydney Star* continued her voyage at a very much reduced speed. But she was not left in peace for long. As the sun came up and Grand Harbour seemed tantalizingly near, two Italian torpedo bombers appeared and began to circle at a discreet distance. Having transferred her troops to the *Nestor*, the *Sydney Star* had no trained gunners to man the four Bofors guns they had left behind, so it was up to Captain Horn and his skeleton crew to do the honours. Their shooting was erratic and mainly ineffective, but it was enough to deter the Italian planes, which ceased to circle the ship and flew away without attacking.

The *Sydney Star*'s ordeal was not yet over. At about 0900 hrs the Italians were back in force with five SM 79s and three Ju 87 dive bombers. The planes wasted no time, mounting a fierce and coordinated attack on the damaged merchantman. Fortunately, HMS *Hermione* now came to her rescue, and the combined gunfire of the three British ships was sufficient to hold the Italians at bay. When two Beaufighters arrived on the scene from Malta the bombers again decided that the odds against them were too great and flew off.

An hour later the island of Malta was in sight, but just as it seemed that the nightmare was over, the air was suddenly full of Italian bombers. One formation of SM 79s tackled the two warships while another formation concentrated on the slow steaming merchantman. The situation worsened when the SM 79s were joined by a flight of Stukas. An eye-witness aboard the *Hermione* described the melee that followed:

> From the bridge I can see the torpedo coming straight for us, leaving a pretty green trail in the blue water. The lookouts shout in chorus and the captain skillfully swings the ship. The torpedo slides past 15 yards to starboard. We lean over and watch it. The bridge where I am is a kind of orderly madhouse of signals, shouts and orders. The commander, pausing a moment between ten other jobs, orders water for the men in the stuffy gun turrets.

> Formations of aircraft are reported but some do not arrive because the Ark's fighters are magnificent.

It seemed that the Italians were determined at all costs to prevent the *Sydney Star* reaching harbour. The contest was finally decided by the arrival of more Beaufighters from Malta, and the intervention of the British fighter/bombers was sufficient to hold off the attackers. Twelve Italian planes were shot down, two were damaged, and two more 'probables' were claimed. It was later learned that one of the Stukas shot down was flown by General Fedrighi, who commanded all Italian airfields in the Mediterranean. In return, six of the Beaufighters from Malta were lost, but the crews of four of these aircraft were rescued.

Meanwhile, the rest of the convoy had reached Malta's Grand Harbour, entering shortly before noon on 24 July. Colin Kitching in HMS *Edinburgh* described the arrival:

> We put on quite a show. The ship's company lined the guard rails, port and starboard. On the quarterdeck the Royal Marines played a selection of patriotic tunes – Rule Britannia, Land of Hope and Glory, Hearts of Oak, and so on. We were given the most tremendous welcome by what must have been the whole population of Valletta. The emotion of the moment was so great that I found that tears were rolling down my cheeks, a reaction which seemed to apply to everyone around me.

Battered, but still afloat, the *Sydney Star* entered Grand Harbour at about 0800 hrs the next morning. Her reception was reported to be 'rapturous'. On arrival, Captain Thomas Horn received the following message from the officers of the convoy's escort:

> THE ROYAL NAVY OFFER YOU THEIR CONGRATULATIONS ON A VERY FINE PIECE OF SEAMANSHIP.

Vice Admiral J. F. Somerville, in overall command of Operation SUBSTANCE, had this to say when it was all over:

> That the operation was successfully carried out is due in no small measure to the behaviour of the merchant ships in the convoy. I had complete confidence that orders given to them by me would be understood and promptly

carried out. Their steadfast and resolute behaviour during air and E-boat attacks was most impressive and encouraging to us all. Particular credit is due to S.S. MELBOURNE STAR'S Master Captain D. R. MacFarlane, Commodore of the convoy, who set a high standard and never failed to appreciate directly what he should do.

CHAPTER TEN

No Surrender

The safe arrival of Operation SUBSTANCE in July 1941 eased the supply situation in Malta for a while, but there was no let-up in the blockade of the island by Axis forces. The intensity of the air attacks on Valetta and Grand Harbour had in fact increased, while the menace of the powerful Italian fleet still dominated the convoy routes. The only supplies reaching the island were being brought in by submarine or the occasional suicide run by destroyers or cruisers.

By mid-September 1941 the besieged island had reached crisis point, and it was decided to attempt to force a substantial supply convoy through. Sailing under the code name of Operation HALBERD, nine fast cargo liners, Blue Funnel Line's *Ajax*, Glen Line's *Breconshire*, Clan Line's *Clan Ferguson* and *Clan MacDonald*, Ellerman City Line's *City of Calcutta* and *City of Lincoln*, Blue Star's *Dunedin Star* and *Imperial Star*, and Union Castle's *Rowallan Castle* were requisitioned for the run. Loaded with 81,000 tons of military stores, fuel and food, along with 2,600 service personnel to reinforce Malta's garrison, these ships sailed from the Clyde on 17 December as part of the large 'Winston Special' convoy WS 11X bound for the Cape. When abreast of the Straits of Gibraltar, the Malta ships turned east into the Mediterranean. Their escort from Gibraltar was Force 'H' under the command of Admiral James Somerville, and consisted of 3 battleships, 1 aircraft carrier, 5 light cruisers, 18 destroyers and 8 submarines. The aircraft carrier, HMS *Ark Royal*, carried a total of 66 combat aircraft.

Faced by such an unprecedented show of force, the Italian fleet decided not to attempt to bar the convoy's way, and made a discreet retreat. Once the British ships reached the Sicilian Narrows, however, they came under heavy attack by a force of 48 Italian high level and torpedo bombers. One of the blockade runners, Blue Star Line's *Imperial Star*, was badly damaged and had to be scuttled, but the others got though to Malta with their cargoes intact. The island was secure for another six months or so.

The success of HALBERD rattled the Axis, who stepped up the air war against Malta, and by the end of 1941 the damage to the island's facilities, especially in the port areas, was crippling the garrison. Three destroyers, three submarines, three mine-sweepers, five tugs, and numerous small craft were sunk at their moorings. Much of the shore installations of Grand Harbour were completely demolished, while 300 civilians were killed and another 350 seriously injured. The resulting chaos led to severe food rationing and Malta ceased to function as a base for air and sea attacks on Rommel's supply convoys. In desperation, it was proposed to attempt another breakthrough.

On 12 February 1942, Convoy MW 9, made up of the three fast cargo liners *Clan Campbell*, *Clan Chattan* and *Rowallan Castle*, each loaded to the gunwales with ammunition, aviation spirit in cans, food and military stores, set out from Alexandria to fight their way through 820 miles of hostile waters to Malta's Grand Harbour. Accompanying the liners were the anti-aircraft cruiser *Carlisle*, the light cruisers *Dido*, *Euryalus* and *Naid*, with the destroyers *Arrow*, *Beaufort*, *Dulverton*, *Griffin*, *Hasty*, *Hurworth*, *Jaguar*, *Jervis* and *Southwold* screening.

The merchant ships chosen for Operation MG 1, as the convoy was designated, were all fast, the *Clan Campbell* and *Clan Chattan* being 17½-knotters from Clan Line's Far East trade, while the *Rowallan Castle*, a cargo/passenger liner of 7,798 tons gross, was classed as 15 knots. All three ships were heavily armed with 40mm Bofors and 20mm Oerlikon guns capable of high angle or low angle use, these being manned by naval gunners. This sixteen-ship convoy, three merchantmen closely guarded by thir-teen warships, positively bristled with anti-aircraft weapons, and any enemy planes foolish enough to tackle it were sure to get a very warm reception.

The first test came forty-eight hours after sailing from Alexandria, when the Luftwaffe pounced on the convoy in force. In an intense running battle that produced more gunsmoke than Trafalgar, the *Clan Chattan* was sunk, and the *Rowallan Castle* so heavily damaged that she was abandoned, later being sunk by friendly fire to avoid her falling into enemy hands. The remain-ing merchantman, *Clan Campbell*, also received heavy damage, but much of this was largely above the waterline, and she was able to take refuge in Tobruk harbour. While sheltering there, her engineers stripped plates from an abandoned Italian warship, and used them to make their own ship seaworthy. *Clan Campbell* returned to Alexandria under her own steam and with her cargo intact.

While Convoy MW 9 did little to improve the situation in Malta, it did serve to signal to the enemy that the island was not going to be left without support. On hearing the news of the failure of yet another relief effort, the Admiralty in London informed Admiral Andrew Cunningham, C-in-C Mediterranean, that his fleet's most important duty in March was to get a convoy through to Malta at all costs. In response, another attempt was made on 20 March.

Convoy MW 10 was made up of four Allied cargo liners carrying between them 26,000 tons of supplies, including a large quantity of aviation spirit and ammunition. Making the run were the 9,776-ton twin-screw motor vessel *Breconshire*, owned by Glen Line of London and requisitioned for the duration as a supply ship by the Royal Navy, the Norwegian-flag *Talabot*, a 6,798-ton cargo/passenger liner of Wilhelm Wilhelmsen, Royal Mail Line's new motor vessel *Pampas* of 5,415 tons gross, and the sole survivor of Convoy MW 9, the 7,255-ton *Clan Campbell.*

The operation began on the night of 19 March 1942, when seven British destroyers, *Avon Vale*, *Beaufort*, *Dulverton*, *Eridge*, *Heythrop*, *Hurworth* and *Southwold* left Alexandria to sweep for any U-boats which might be lurking along MW 10's planned route.

On the afternoon of the 20th, the destroyer flotilla was off the Libyan coast 10 miles north-east of Bardia, when *U-652*, commanded by *Kapitänleutnant* Georg-Werner Fraatz, torpedoed HMS *Heythrop*. The destroyer suffered major damage, including the loss of her after gun mounting; her port propeller was disabled and because of damage to one of her boilers her pumps were unable to cope with the water pouring into the engine room. Fifteen of *Heythrop*'s crew lost their lives in the torpedoing and its aftermath. The crippled destroyer was taken in tow by HMS *Eridge*, but before many miles had been covered *Heythrop* began to sink, and she was scuttled. The remaining destroyers then put into Tobruk to refuel before returning to Alexandria. Their mission had been largely in vain, and extremely costly.

The four loaded merchant ships comprising Convoy MW 10 sailed from Alexandria at 0800 hrs on 20 March, escorted by the destroyers *Hasty, Havoc, Hero, Lively, Sikh* and *Zulu*. The weather on leaving port was partially overcast, with a fresh wind and rough seas; miserable for those on watch above deck, but offering good cover for the ships. Later that evening, the cruisers *Cleopatra, Dido* and *Euryalus*, the destroyers *Jervis, Kelvin, Kingston and Kipling* put to sea under cover of darkness. The two squadrons met at a pre-arranged rendezvous off Tobruk early on the 21st, where they were later joined by the destroyers *Avon Vale, Beaufort, Dulverton, Eridge, Hurworth* and *Southwold*. Around 0800 hrs that morning, the cruiser *Penelope* and the destroyer *Legion* arrived from Malta. This large assembly of ships, four merchantmen surrounded by five light cruisers and seventeen destroyers, under the command of Rear Admiral Sir Philip Vian, then set off on the last and most dangerous leg of the voyage to Malta.

Six hours later, lookouts aboard the cruiser *Euryalus* sighted the outriders of the Italian fleet, the sighting coinciding with the arrival overhead of a large number of German and Italian aircraft, which immediately dived to attack. A report of the mayhem that followed written by Chief Officer R. E. Slinn of the *Pampas* is surprisingly precise and calm. Lunch was not interrupted:

> At 1000 on the 22nd the battle began. The first attack was delivered by Italian torpedo bombers, and this was repelled. About 9 aircraft took part. The second attack about a dozen bombers came over just before lunch, these also being Italian torpedo bombers. We had a lull for about half an hour, during which we had our lunch, and after that the attacks were almost continuous, the Italians being joined by German Ju 88s. We received a signal from Admiral Vian soon after lunch that a formation of enemy dive bombers had been sighted bearing 320° to 060° and within 10 minutes they were on us, but just before they arrived we sighted the masts of strange vessels on the horizon which upon inspection proved to be the Italian Battle Fleet. Admiral Vian at once made a signal to our ships and they went off to fight, leaving the convoy with 4 Hunt class destroyers only to meet the dive bombers. Our ships laid a thick smoke screen as they went off, we

Booth Line's *Clement* (State Library of Queensland)

Pocket battleship *Admiral Graf Spee* (US Naval Heritage Command)

Dunkirk – waiting for evacuation (Military-History.org)

Clan Macalister with heavy-lift derricks (Clan Line Archives)

ALCs discharged by *Clan Macalister* (Clan Line Archives)

Remains of *Clan Macalister* at low water (Clan Line Archives)

Turakina (National Library of Australia)

Captain James Boyd Laird (Auckland Museum)

Italian MTB (Unknown photographer of the Regia Marina)

Italian Savoia Marchetti SM 79 torpedo bomber

The end of the *Waimarama* (Royal Navy photographer)

The *Ohio* enters Grand Harbour (Lieutenant E. Cook)

Melbourne Star (Blue Star Line)

Union Castle Line poster (Union Castle Line)

Bofors gun mounted on
deck of *Melbourne Star*
(Lieutenant J. A. Hampton)

Malta convoy under attack (From a painting by Oswald Longfield Brett)

merchant vessels laid our smoke floats and turned away to 080°. We saw terrific bursts of firing away to the north for about 20 minutes, but meanwhile the enemy aircraft had started to attack, the enemy plan evidently being to draw off our escorts to meet the Italian fleet, leaving the merchantmen to the dive bombers.

At 1610 we received another signal from Admiral Vian – 'I have repelled the enemy battle fleet.' Then Cleopatra returned. In the meantime the enemy had apparently found out the extent of our force and decided to try and intercept us before reaching Malta. The Commodore, on receipt of Admiral Vian's signal, gave us a course to the North. The smoke screen hid us, and just before dark on the 22nd we again saw salvos of 15" shells bursting about a mile to the northward so we turned away once more. The dive bombing had continued throughout the afternoon and evening until dark, all the merchant ships put up a terrific barrage, the Breconshire being fitted with pom-poms, and no hits were scored by the enemy. Our gunners shot down one Savoia bomber at about 1600 during the afternoon. It came in low over the TALABOT, and straight for us at a height of about 50 feet. We fired but it continued on its course so that we could not miss. We could see the bullets pouring into him, he banked, did not release his torpedo, but went straight down into the sea, the pilot probably being killed. I think it was brought down by shells from an Oerlikon and possibly the starboard Hotchkiss on the bridge. The destroyer astern of us hit a Ju 88 practically amidships, blowing it to pieces.

On the night of 22nd/23rd the weather was very heavy, and as we turned away from the enemy we were going full speed – about 16 knots – right into it, so that it became impossible to man the forward guns as they were under water. Away to the north the horizon was just one huge red glare, and we heard afterwards from officers of HM ships that they had fired many torpedoes at the Italian fleet. We were left with just one Hunt-class destroyer and after dark she signalled with her night lamp 'If you should meet the enemy during the night, turn away, make as much smoke as possible, and I will endeavour to hold him.' This, with the Italian battle fleet at sea – it certainly scared me a bit.

Looking back over the years, it is hard to imagine the dire situation facing these four merchant ships.

During the bad weather, which was really bad, we lost the destroyer, the convoy had dispersed, and at daylight on the 23rd we were alone, when at 0730 we were attacked by a formation of Ju 88s. One of the formation dived at us from a height of 3–4000 feet, releasing his bombs just before he pulled out of his dive at 1000 feet, and firing with all his guns at the same time. The armour plating of the gun shields was not penetrated, but the bullets pierced the bulwarks. The enemy scored two direct hits on our ship, the first bomb falling on No.1 hold, and the second on No.2 hold, which was full of benzine, but fortunately neither bomb exploded. They disintegrated, and later on we found the tailfins, which were marked with the figures 602. Our gunners were firing all the time and one Ju 88 was seen making off with flames streaming out of her, but no smoke. Ten minutes later another plane dived at us and released a salvo of 5 bombs under our stern which almost lifted the ship out of the water, and after that we were subjected to a machine-gun attack by a Messerschmidt which wounded three of our crew at the guns.

We arrived at Malta on Monday the 23rd, where we found that we had all arrived safely except the CLAN CAMPBELL. Our gunners during all this time had put up a marvellous show. The three merchant seamen who were hit were knocked down by the impact, but in spite of their wounds, they all jumped up and continued to fire their guns until the action was over. One of them, the Bos'un, even grumbled because he could not ram his gun properly, his boots being full of blood from a wound in his leg.

While this drama of the merchant ships was being enacted, Admiral Vian and his ships had steamed boldly to meet the Italian fleet, which consisted of the 30-knot battleship *Littorio*, armed with nine 15-inch and twelve 6-inch guns, the heavy cruiser *Gorizia* with eight 8-inch and sixteen 4-inch guns, and the light cruiser *Giovanni delle Bande Nere* with four twin 6-inch and three twin 3.9-inch guns. Screening them were ten destroyers with multiple 4-inch guns. All these ships had speeds in excess of 30 knots, and both the *Littorio* and her cruisers were protected by heavy armour. In firepower the Italians held all the aces, but their commitment to do battle was again questionable.

The weather had been deteriorating by the hour, and by the time it was dark the opposing ships were slamming into short steep seas as hard and unyielding as brick walls. The British narrow-hulled destroyers were taking the worst punishment, pitching and rolling violently, their decks constantly awash with angry green seas. This was a face of the Mediterranean never shown in the glossy brochures lining the shelves of the travel agents.

The two sides met head-on in the gathering dusk, and Vian's cruisers began to swap shell for shell with the big guns of the Italian fleet, while his destroyers were all the time probing, making suicidal dashes through the smoke to launch their torpedoes. HMS *Cleopatra* was first to be hit, a shell from the light cruiser *Giovanni delle Bande Nere* killing sixteen of her crew and causing extensive damage. The cruisers *Euryalus* and *Penelope* were straddled, probably by the *Littorio*'s secondary armament, but the damage was not severe. *Littorio* also hit the destroyer *Kingston*, killing fifteen of her crew and starting a fire in her engine room, causing serious damage on deck, and one of her boiler rooms was flooded. She was forced to retire from the fight, but was able to reach port under her own steam. Another British destroyer, HMS *Havoc* fell victim to the Italian battleships' shells, losing eight men and sustaining heavy damage on deck, while her sisters *Lance*, *Legion*, *Lively* and *Sikh* all suffered in their attempts to torpedo the Italian ships, and were also forced to put into Tobruk for repairs.

Lieutenant Robert Ritchie, in the destroyer HMS *Sikh* commented:

> We had been bombed regularly since leaving Alexandria. We were usually at action stations from dawn to dusk with a few rest breaks. We closed up at about 1400 and were kept fully occupied for four hours. The ship was

doing about 28 knots into a head sea. The ammunition chute of 'A' gun was open to the sea. We were passing ammunition with water cascading down on us. Our mess deck lockers were floating around because the water was as high as the mess deck coaming. I think we were more afraid of the lockers than the 15" shells being fired at us by the Littorio.

Reports show that in what has now come to be known as the Second Battle of Sirte, the Italian fleet fired a total of 1,511 shells of all calibres, while Vian's cruisers and destroyers replied with some 2,800 rounds, plus 38 torpedoes. Contrary to expectations, the Italians showed no hesitation to fight, and despite their lack of radar, hit the British ships hard. In return, they suffered very little damage or casualties. If they had persisted, they could have won the day, but the weather and the sheer agression of the British warships in the end proved too much for them. Led by the *Littorio*, they broke off the action and fled into the night making no attempt to get at the merchant ships.

On the other side of the smoke screen the *Clan Campbell* was in serious trouble. Second Officer John Holman explains:

On 23rd March at 0900 we were picked up by two reconnaissance aircraft. They were flying at a height of about 3–4000 feet just out of range of our guns. One of them dropped 4 flares; when we saw this we called up the destroyer and received the answer 'these planes are hostile'. These aircraft circled round and round until at 1040, when in a position 8 miles east of Malta we were attacked by a Ju 88 bomber. The aircraft came out of the sun flying at a height of about 5000 feet; he was only 1–2 miles away from us when we first heard the roar of his engines and we therefore had very little time to do anything before we were attacked.

The aircraft came straight towards us from the sun approaching on our starboard quarter, and the Master immediately ordered the helm to be put hard to starboard. The aircraft dropped two bombs, the first hit the water on the starboard side, jumped right over the ship and exploded in the water on the port side.

The aircraft then circled round the ship, and again approached us from starboard to port, but further astern than on the first attack. Two bombs were dropped which fell close to the ship abreast of No.5 hold on the starboard side, lifting the ship out of the water.

We opened fire with all our guns but this did not seem to affect the attacking plane. We were definitely hitting the plane with our fire, but it flew off without apparent damage after the attack. The guns' crews behaved very well indeed, but they experienced trouble with one of the Oerlikon guns. We got some more ammunition in Alexandria, but it was American and would not fit very well. The men tried mixing the ammunition with what they already had, but when it came to the American ammunition the gun jammed, and the men could not get it to work again.

The force of the explosion from the bombs broke the propeller shaft and knocked the 3" gun overboard. Water immediately gushed into the engine room through the bulkhead from No.4 and the ship commenced to sink very rapidly.

I got away two boats on the port side, which was the lee side. The sea at the time was very rough with the wind WNW Force 6/7. One boat was lowered on the starboard side but as the after fall was not released in time, a number of the occupants were thrown into the water. The boat was eventually released and the men who had been thrown out were picked up.

Several of the crew jumped into the water just before the ship sank and they were picked up, but I do not know what happened to the men who are missing, they were not killed by the explosion and I think they must have been drowned.

We were picked up by HMS *Eridge* after we had been in the boats about 20 minutes. She circled round for about 1½ hours searching for survivors. We were not bombed during this time, but were attacked on the way back to Malta.

The ship sank stern-first about 20 minutes after being bombed. Some of the crew were still on board at the time, and they said that when the ship sank they were not pulled down by the suction but were pushed off into the water.

We had a Liaison Officer, Commander Blackman, on board at the time, who was later rescued. He was with the Captain at the end and has no idea what became of him. The Captain behaved wonderfully throughout the attack on the previous day, and people speaking to him after the bombing said that he was very overwrought and did not seem to know what he was doing. Throughout the attack on 22 March the Captain undoubtedly saved the ship over and over again, and being a rather slower ship than the rest of the convoy, we were slightly astern and were singled out and bombed continually.

It was a sad end for the men of the *Clan Campbell*. They had been through the gates of hell in their attempt to bring succour to Malta, and they had lost their ship and their Captain. One would have thought that those who survived would have been welcomed home as heroes. It was not to be. Second Officer John Holman recalls:

We remained in Malta 6 days and came back to England in HMS *Aurora*. When we arived in Liverpool our Owners had not been notified of our arrival, and so we were met by the immigration authorities and the Shipwrecked Mariners' Association [Society].

A signal was sent to Liverpool early in the morning of the day we arrived to say who was on board, but when we arrived alongside the landing stage about 1315 our Owners still knew nothing of our arrival.

We had no money and were trying to get the Paymaster to forward us some money which he would later draw from Clan Line. We were, however, given £2 each by the Shipping Federation and also a warrant from the Shipwrecked Mariners' Association.

For the remaining merchantmen, the naval supply vessel *Breconshire*, the Norwegian in exile, *Talabot,* and Royal Mail's *Pampas*, it was a fight to the finish. Their guns were still running hot when they reached Valletta's Grand Harbour on the morning of 28 March, and the end to their ordeal was still not in sight. Chief Officer Slinn of the *Pampas* later wrote:

> We had continual daylight bombing whilst in Grand Harbour from 23rd to the 26th March. On the 24th, out of 8 hours working time we lost 4 hours 36 minutes for unloading owing to the bombing. We also lost time in unloading as several of our derricks had been put out of action. The weather during these three days was fine, with good visibility but on the 26th there was consider-able low cloud. The first day in the harbour the enemy tried Ju 88s, but these did not prove successful, most of the bombs falling on the town of Valletta, so the next day they sent over the Ju 87 dive bombers which plastered the harbour with bombs, so that they were bound to hit something. I was ashore at the time, but between noon and 1430 BMT on the 26th there was a fierce attack by Stukas and the *Pampas* was hit. A bomb went down her funnel and burst at the base, wrecking the accommoda-tion amidships and setting it on fire. We returned to the ship and fought the fire, but found that the holds were filling and the engine room was soon flooded. The vessel must have been damaged also by the many near-misses which fell around her, and at about 1600 she touched the bottom and we had to abandon her. The enemy sank the *Talabot* the same afternoon. The *Breconshire* had a bomb down her funnel on the first day in harbour, she was beached, but during the attacks on the following days the Stukas made her one of their principal targets and eventually she sank, so that all four ships of our convoy had gone.

And so it had all been in vain, the four gauntlet runners sunk, the escorting ships badly mauled, a great deal of blood shed, and all for the handful of cargo that was landed under fire by those ships that got through.

CHAPTER ELEVEN

Union Castle at War

In those carefree days between the two world wars, before air travel came within reach of the masses, there was only one way to go to the Cape and that was by Union Castle.

Every Thursday afternoon, at precisely 4.00 pm, one of Union Castle's lavender-hulled mail ships would leave Southampton for Cape Town. At the same time another of the company steamers sailed from Cape Town on the return voyage north. Some six days later, weather permitting, the two vessels would dip ensigns as they crossed off the coast of Sierra Leone. Invariably, the passenger accommodation of both ships would be fully booked.

By present day cruise-ship standards, the Union Castle liners would be regarded as somewhat basic. Their accommodation was adequate but not lavish, the food was 4-star hotel, there was a small swimming pool and miles of scrubbed teak wooden decks to walk, but for as little as ten guineas one way – third-class of course – who could want more? The company's advertising blurb says it all:

> The 6,000-mile journey to or from South Africa can be a
> leisurely, refreshing holiday in itself. You sail, in the main,
> through warm, sunlit seas. It's relaxation and enjoyment
> all the way, backed up, of course, by the traditional,
> friendly Union Castle service.

There was another side to Union Castle. In addition to the passenger/mail ships the company operated a number of smaller cargo/passenger ships which sailed every Friday from London on an advertised service to South and East Africa, calling at Ascension and St. Helena on the outward passage, and returning via Suez. One such ship was the 7,798-ton *Richmond Castle*.

Built in 1939 by Harland & Wolff of Belfast, the *Richmond Castle* was powered by an 8-cylinder diesel engine which gave her a service speed of 16 knots. The dark clouds of war were already gathering over Europe when the *Richmond Castle* left the shipyard, and all thoughts of the quiet life on the Cape run were abandoned. She was eminently suited to supply wartime Britain with food, and to that end, at the behest of the Government, she was taken out of service and converted to a meat carrier, with all holds refrigerated.

Under the command of 60-year-old Captain Thomas Goldstone, and manned by a British crew of sixty-two, the *Richmond Castle* became a regular on the South American meat run, crossing the Atlantic every few months with 5,000 tons of frozen Agentinian beef. She sailed alone, relying on her speed and the 4-inch gun mounted at her stern to run the gauntlet of Hitler's U-boats.

For a while, the *Richmond Castle* bore a charmed life, unbothered by U-boats, surface raiders, or the 4-engined Focke-Wulf Kondors that sometimes haunted the grey wastes of the broad Atlantic. Ironically, when the challenge came it was not from the enemy, but from one of her own. Many years later, John Cutliffe, who was a young cadet in the *Richmond Castle* at the time of the incident, wrote:

> Our orders took us around the eastern tip of Brazil at Cape Recife and then in a NW'ly direction towards the Caribbean, the idea being to keep the maximum distance between us and our U-boat friends, now operating out of French Atlantic Coast ports, for as long as possible. During the daylight hours we followed a series of zig-zag courses, but at night we steered a straight course without navigation lights. We had been routed from Point 'A' to Point 'B', but what we didn't know was the some idiot in the Admiralty had routed another British ship from 'B' to 'A'. On a dark night, about 0100, there was a report from our forward lookout that he could see something dead ahead and so it proved. Under such circumstances, i.e. vessels meeting 'end-on', the law dictates that each vessel shall alter course to starboard to pass down the port side of the other. This we did – but to our utter horror she turned in the opposite direction. The next 30–40 seconds were without any doubt whatsoever, the most frightening and horrendous of my whole life. Once committed, there was nothing that either ship could do to avoid certain disaster. With an approach speed of 30

knots we ploughed into the starboard side of her No.2 hatch, and as she maintained her way past us we swept away her bridge, much of her starboard accommodation and starboard boats with our forecastle. The noise and feel of 30,000 tons of ships and cargo crashing into each other at that speed was unbelievable. Men were screaming in pain and fear.

The other vessel turned out to be the British vessel *City of Bangalore*, outward bound to Cape Town with a cargo mainly destined for the armed forces. Both ships were severely damaged, but remarkably had remained afloat. Throughout the remainder of the night we managed to rescue most of the other vessel's crew, but a number of her Indian crew were never found. At daylight the next day we started to attempt to tow the *City of Bangalore* towards Trinidad, the nearest friendly port. It was a dangerous task, as even had we been successful progress would have been painfully slow. After several attempts the operation proved impossible due to the severity of the damage she had suffered. After consultation the two captains reluctantly decided that in the best interests of saving something from the incident we would sink the *City of Bangalore* by gunfire. I had been the junior on the bridge at the time of the accident, the 2nd Officer being the O.O.W. And it so happened that he doubled as the Gunnery Officer and I as the Gunlayer on our 4.7 inch gun. It fell to the two of us to give the 'coup de grace' with six shells along her waterline – a sad task.

When he wrote the above, many years after the war, John Cutliffe's memory played him false. Records show that the other ship involved in the collision was not the *City of Bangalore*, but the 6,067-ton steamer *Bangalore*, owned by the Hain Steamship Company of London, and that she was bound for Hong Kong via the Cape. Few details of this ship and her crew are known, but it is clear from John Cutliffe's narrative that she was to blame for the collision. Article 18 of the Regulations for Preventing Collisions at Sea, which still holds good until this day, states, *When two steam vessels are meeting end on, or nearly end on, so as to involve risk of collision, each shall alter her course to starboard, so that each may pass on the port side of the other.* For some reason unknown, when she sighted the *Richmond Castle* on that dark night in the Atlantic, the *Bangalore* ignored the rule and made an alteration to port, thus inviting disaster. An end-on collision at sea is every watch-keeping officer's worst nightmare, and in the 1940s, with no radar and running without navigation lights, it was a danger all too frequently faced.

This unfortunate meeting with the *Bangalore* left the *Richmond Castle* afloat, but with a badly mangled bow, and Captain Goldstone wisely opted to abandon the voyage and put into the nearest port where a temporary repair could be effected. This was Port of Spain in the Caribbean island of Trinidad, then some 1,200 miles to the north-west. Steaming at reduced speed to avoid further damage to her bows, the *Richmond Castle* reached Trinidad five days later. There her bows were shored up and she was then routed north to Halifax, Nova Scotia, to await an eastbound convoy across the Atlantic. However, after further consideration it was decided that, even in company with a slow convoy, the *Richmond Castle* in her present state would be unwise to challenge the great ocean. Goldstone was ordered to make for New York, where his cargo would be discharged into another British ship. Thereafter, he was to return south to the Gulf of Mexico, where a more permanent repair to the damaged bow section would be carried out at Galveston, Texas.

It was late November 1941 when the *Richmond Castle*, her bows completely rebuilt, returned to New York to load another cargo for the United Kingdom. The long and unexpected sojourn in the Americas had been a welcome break from the horrors of war for Captain Goldstone and his crew. The bright lights, the well-stocked shops and the warm hospitality shown to them by people on shore had been beyond expectation. However, while they had been thus indulged, storm clouds were gathering in the Pacific.

The United States and Japan had been on the brink of war for decades over the latter's aggressive meddling in China and neighbouring countries, where a great deal of American money was invested. Following the Japanese invasion of French Indo-China in June 1941, America imposed sanctions on Japan, which included a ban on the export of all American oil to Japan. This had very serious consequences for the Japanese, who had no oil of their own, and they began to cast envious eyes at the Dutch East Indies, which were fabulously rich in oil and rubber, both sorely needed by the Japanese military. Plans were laid to invade Java and Sumatra, but before any action was embarked upon in the Pacific, the Japanese High Command knew they would first have to deal with the powerful US Pacific fleet based in Pearl Harbor on the island of Hawaii.

On 26 November 1941 a Japanese strike force, consisting of six aircraft carriers and their attendant destroyers under the command of Admiral Isoroku Yamamoto, left Japan and sailed south-east. Eight days later, they reached a position close north-west of Hawaii. Reconnaissance aircraft sent up from the carriers reported that the entire US Pacific fleet was anchored in or around their base at Pearl Harbor.

The attack began shortly before 8 o'clock on the morning of Sunday, 7 December, when Pearl Harbor was at breakfast. Church parades were planned for later in the morning and although the garrison was supposedly on alert no one was prepared for the horrors that were to come.

Without warning the azure blue skies over the harbour suddenly turned black as the first wave of Yamamoto's carrier-borne fighters and bombers came roaring in. A hail of bombs, torpedoes and machine-gun bullets rained down on the anchored ships, swept inland to engulf the naval base and its nearby airfield, bringing widespread death and destruction before a single gun could be manned in retaliation. The second wave of Japanese planes followed close in the slipstream of the first, a total of 360 aircraft being involved.

Four of the US Navy's finest battleships were sunk at their moorings, while four others were severely damaged. The Japanese bombs also sank three cruisers, three destroyers, an anti-aircraft training ship and a minelayer. On shore, the garrison's only airfield was a scene of complete devastation, 188 aircraft being destroyed on the ground. In all, a total of 2,403 US service men and civilians were killed, while 1,178 others were injured. On the other side, the Japanese lost 29 aircraft and 64 men. And all this happened while America and Japan were officially at peace, and representatives of the two countries were still negotiating. Twenty-four hours later on 8 December, President Roosevelt addressed Congress, stating, 'Yesterday, December 7,

1941 – a date which will live in infamy – the United States of America was suddenly and deliberately attacked by naval and air forces of the Empire of Japan.' That being said, Roosevelt proceeded to declare war on Japan.

John Cutcliffe commented:

> We sailed on a fateful day, the 8th December 1941, the day after the Japanese attack on Pearl Harbor, and the day that the USA actually declared war. It was also my 19th birthday. Having spent the three previous months in the USA we were all too well aware that, while there was great sympathy with the plight of the UK, and a willingness on many citizens' part to help where they could, there was no discernible will to enter the war on our side. The Japanese attack proved to be the most stupid thing that they could have done as it catapulted the USA straight into the war by just this one fateful action.

Again running alone at full speed, the *Richmond Castle* crossed the Atlantic unmolested, after which she returned to Argentina to load another cargo of frozen meat for the UK. This was also delivered safely. And this was at a time when, despite the added protection the US Navy was providing in the North Atlantic, the U-boats were sinking 100 Allied ships a month. The stress experienced by Captain Goldstone and his men was immense, but they were by now experienced gauntlet runners, and they made light of it. Unfortunately, their charmed life was about to come to an end.

Reiner Dierksen, a career merchant service officer, joined Germany's Reichsmarine in 1933, and by March 1941 had risen to the rank of Flotilla Commander in minesweepers. At that point he transferred to the U-boat Arm, and was given his first command in December of that year. She was the brand-new Type IXC long-range boat *U-176*.

Built in the Deschimag yard at Bremen, *U-176* was of 1,120 tons displacement surfaced, 252 feet long and 22 feet in the beam. Her twin-screw diesels gave her a range of 15,480 miles at 10 knots when surfaced, while she was able to remain submerged for 64 miles at 4 knots on her electric motors. Her armament consisted of six 21-inch torpedo tubes with a supply of twenty-two torpedoes, a 4-inch deck gun with 180 rounds, a 1.5-inch anti-aircraft gun and twin 20mm Flak 30 cannon.

After extensive training in the Baltic, *U-176* sailed from Kiel on 21 July 1942, just three days after the *Richmond Castle* left Montevideo bound for Avonmouth with yet another cargo of frozen meat. As had become the norm, she was sailing unescorted, relying on her superior speed to get her through the U-boat packs. Seventeen days later she was in mid-ocean, having covered much of the Atlantic from south to north without a single enemy sighting.

Unknown to Captain Goldstone, his run of good luck was about to end. Reiner Dierksen had sighted the *Richmond Castle* before dawn that day, and had been stalking her at periscope depth ever since. By the late forenoon, *U-176* was in position and Dierksen prepared to fire. John Cutliffe remembers:

> Our charmed life was not to last. We were struck by two torpedoes at 1125 on 4/8/42 in 50° 25′ N 35° 05′ W about 750 miles to the east of Newfoundland, and the ship sank at 1132 (just 7 minutes later). We learned many years afterwards that we had been attacked by *U176* under the command of Lt-Com Reiner Dierksen, in fact we were the first vessel to be sunk by *U176* and Dierksen. . . . Three out of four lifeboats were launched, but one (No.2 Boat) capsized in the process and most of the equipment was lost. The boat was later righted and was the one in which I spent the next nine days.

Able Seaman Angus Murray gave a more detailed description of the torpedoing:

> About noon there was a terrific explosion. Everything in my cabin fell in pieces around me. I was terrified until I remembered how the Lord had helped me previously. I recovered my composure and put on some warm clothing. I took my Bible, my two watches and my lifebelt from my locker and headed for the open deck. The sea was entering No.4 hatch as I made my way with difficulty to the boat deck.
>   I assisted in lowering the last lifeboat as the ship heeled over, sinking. I shinned down a fall and swam to the

lifeboat. It was waterlogged. We had to swim to a raft as the lifeboat capsized. It took quite an effort to right the boat and to bail her out. A lot of its equipment, including the sails, food and water, was lost. There were eighteen of us, including the Chief Officer, aboard.

Both John Cutcliffe and Angus Murray remarked on the humane treatment they received at the hands of Reiner Dierksen. Murray wrote:

> The U-boat which torpedoed our ship surfaced. They showed us great kindness, giving us field dressings for each boat, and they told us the nearest landfall was Newfoundland. They waved goodbye to us as they submerged.

Cutcliffe enlarged on this:

> At about midday on August 4, 1942, I was one of some 62 surviving crew clustered in and around three ship's lifeboats, one of which was overturned, about 750 miles to the east of Newfoundland. We had just watched our torpedoed ship, *Richmond Castle*, which had been homeward bound with a cargo of Argentine meat, slide stern-first beneath the Atlantic.
>
> Coming up alongside us was a brand new *U-176* under the command of Lt-Cdr Reiner Dierksen. Rumours abounded then that survivors were being shot up by German submariners, and we could see that not only were the sub's main armaments manned, but several crew members were also carrying sub-machine guns. We watched its approach with some apprehension.
>
> But Dierksen shouted for the boats to close on him. He asked if there were any injured and passed over field dressings. Tinned butter, biscuits and other foodstuffs were passed down to the boats, and we were given the course and distance to the nearest land. Dierksen said that he would try to send out an SOS message for us, and wished us 'Cheerio, goodbye and good luck' before proceeding on his way.

It is worth mentioning here that out of the 3,500 plus Allied merchant ships sunk by the U-boats in the Second World

War, there were only eight alleged cases of crew being fired upon while they were abandoning ship. Of these only one was proven, that of the Greek steamer *Peleus*, sunk by *U-852* in the South Atlantic on 13 March 1944.

The 4,695-ton *Peleus*, commanded by Captain Minas Mavris, was bound in ballast from Freetown to Buenos Aires, when she was sighted and torpedoed by *U-852*, which was then on its way to take up a patrol in the Indian Ocean. The Greek ship broke up and sank within three minutes, but most of her crew survived by taking to the rafts.

U-852's commander, *Kapitänleutnant* Heinz-Wilhelm Eck, anxious that the U-boat's position should not be given away, ordered the survivors of the *Peleus* to be killed and her rafts destroyed. For the next five hours *U-852* cruised amongst the wreckage, machine-gunning the survivors and destroying their rafts with hand grenades. Of the *Peleus*'s crew of thirty-five, only three survived to be picked up by a passing Portuguese merchantman some four weeks later.

On 2 May 1945, *U-852* ran aground on a reef in the Indian Ocean and Eck and his crew were taken prisoner. When the war was over, Heinz-Wilhelm Eck and four others appeared before the War Crimes Commission and were found guilty of murder. Eck and two of his officers were sentenced to death and hanged.

At the height of the U-boat war in the Atlantic rumour, no doubt fuelled by Government propaganda, ran rife regarding the indiscriminate machine-gunning of torpedoed ships' crews. In fact, in most cases survivors reported on how well they were treated by their attackers. As many of the U-boat commanders involved were ex-merchant seamen, this is perhaps not surprising. Reports of U-boat men threatening the lifeboats with sub-machine guns when survivors were being questioned are widespread, but this again can be put down to propaganda by the other side. U-boat crews were warned of the danger of hand grenades being thrown on board from boats as they came alongside.

Fifty survivors from her crew of sixty got away from the *Richmond Castle* before she sank. Amongst the survivors were two seamen from the Outer Hebrides, Able Seaman John Maciver and Able Seaman Angus Murray, both men who had been handling small boats in heavy seas since childhood. Of Murray, Second Radio Officer Peter Franklin said, 'He was the only fellow in the boat who knew anything about small boats, and our Chief Officer had the sense to let him get on with it. His soft gentle manner gave us confidence and hope.' Some years later, Murray himself wrote:

> There were eighteen of us, including the Chief Officer, aboard. John Maciver was in another boat with the Second Officer. The Captain was in the third lifeboat.
>
> It was decided that the boats should make for New-foundland. During the night a westerly gale blew up and we lost sight of each other. It was bitterly cold. We fixed up a sea anchor with a couple of buckets, an oar, and a rope we recovered from among the debris floating on the sea where the ship had sunk.
>
> Sometime during the following forenoon we sighted the other lifeboats. The Second Officer's boat approached us and told us the Captain was still heading for Newfoundland, but he himself was going to try for Ireland. They took us in tow as we had no sail. It was slow going, so after more consultations with the Chief Officer, I started to make a sail with blankets. I sewed two together with rope yarn. We hoisted this onto a ten-foot high flagstaff which we had recovered. It was crude but useful, as was a lugsail fashioned out of a 6 x 3 foot piece of wood with an oar for a mast. In fact it worked so well that we were going as fast as the other boat so we decided to sail independently. Before part-ing, the Second Officer shared food with us as we were running short and anticipating a three-week sail to land. We soon lost sight of each other.

Facing what must have seemed like unsurmountable odds, strictly rationed with food and water, the survivors coaxed their boat with its makeshift sails ever westwards. They were cold, wet and miserable, but by massaging each other's hands and feet with fish oil, a can of which was carried in lifeboats during the war for this specific purpose, they avoided frostbite.

Progress was painfully slow and on Sunday, 10 August, their sixth day in the boat, the wind and sea rose and they were forced to heave-to and lie to their improvised sea anchor. Fortunately, by dawn on the 11th the weather had moderated and sail was re-hoisted. The only navigation aids in the boat were an unstable magnetic compass and a small-scale Atlantic chart that had been rescued from the flooded locker in the bows of the boat, and all navigation, which was in the hands of Chief Officer Walter Gibb, was 'by guess and by God', or as the books call it, 'dead reckoning'. However, the greatest challenge the survivors faced was without doubt the cruel North Atlantic weather. John Cutliffe, who was also in the boat, later remarked:

> The principal cause of the problems we experienced was the lack of almost any protection from the weather. This meant that with constant exposure to the continuous wind and spray our body temperatures dropped dramatically, and that takes its toll, physically and mentally. Hypothermia, or 'exposure' as it was called in those days, is an insidious and deadly enemy, killing you slowly and surely. Exhaustion sets in, the will to live goes, and the mental processes fall apart . . . In our boat we had managed to get hold of the canvas cover of the potato locker from the boat deck which we found floating around amongst all the other debris from the ship. Without any doubt that rough and ready windbreak provided just sufficient shelter to play a significant part in saving the lives of all of us, especially those of us who were not properly dressed for the occasion (I was dressed in shirt and shorts!). It is significant that although we were the least well provided for in many ways because of the boat overturning we were the only boat in which there were no deaths. . . .

Out of the *Richmond Castle*'s crew of 64 there were no casualties caused by Reiner Dierksen's torpedo. The losses came afterwards, as fourteen men, including Captain Tom Goldstone, died of exposure in the open boats. The survivors were picked up by the Irish steamer *Irish Pine*, the British troopship *Hororata* and the Flower-class corvette *Sunflower*. Of the ordeal they had survived John Cutliffe wrote:

> Not surprisingly, considering we had come through 9 days of severe weather and very testing conditions, including a full Atlantic gale in a small ill-equipped open

boat, some of the crew were in such bad shape when we arrived in 'Derry' that they remained in hospital for some while. I managed to hide most of my problems – I had 13 boils on one leg, 11 on the other, and 3 on my right arm. Both feet were so swollen that I had to wear slippers which had to be cut open in order to get my feet into them – as I was determined to get back to my home in Ilfracombe, North Devon just as soon as I could. I started on my long journey by train/ferry within a couple of days of landing there.

The *Richmond Castle* had been Reiner Dierksen's first success with *U-176*. The two went on to sink a total of eleven Allied merchantmen totalling 53,307 tons in three Atlantic patrols. *U-176* sailed fom Lorient on her third patrol on 6 April 1943, crossing the Atlantic to the Caribbean Sea, where the U-boats were enjoying their second 'happy time'. While she was nearing her new hunting ground, Dierksen received a signal from Berlin informing him that he had been promoted to *Korvettenkapitän*, the equivalent of Lieutenant Commander in the Royal Navy and a much-coveted rank.

Buoyed up by his promotion, Dierksen began attacking the small convoys that plied the Caribbean. On 13 May he sank the 2,249-ton US tanker *Nickeliner*, loaded with 3,400 tons of ammonia water, and in the same convoy the 1,983-ton Cuban molasses tanker *Mambi*. Two days later, *U-176* was submerged while stalking a small Havana-bound convoy escorted by three Cuban submarine chasers, when she was sighted by a patrolling US Navy reconnaissance aircraft. The plane dropped a smoke float to mark the U-boat's position, and contacted the convoy's escort. *CS 13*, one of the Cuban submarine chasers, commanded by Lieutenant Mario Ramirez Delgado, immediately homed in on the smoke marker and attacked with depth charges. Caught unawares, *U-176* went to the bottom with all on board.

In the archive *WW2 People's War* the following entry appears:

In early January 2002, a scientific team searching off the coast of Cuba for sunken Spanish galleons stumbled across the wreck of a World War Two U-boat missing since the 15th of May 1943, and now intend to return to the site to make a documentary film of the wreckage. The exploration will be difficult, as the vessel lies at a depth of 800 to 900 metres and will require the use of deep-sea video equipment and remote operated vehicles. The U-boat also still contains the crew of 53 submariners, entombed inside the steel hull.

CHAPTER TWELVE

Last Battle for Malta

In high summer the Mediterranean is at its best; mirror-calm seas shimmering under a flawless blue sky, a breeze that is no more than a tease, and with just enough haze on the horizon to provide cover for a submarine idling on the surface. It was the latter aspect that pleased 29-year-old *Kapitänleutnant* Helmut Rosenbaum most as he relaxed in the conning tower of *U-73* soaking up the warm sun on that morning in late July 1942. This was the third day *U-73* had spent marking time south of the Balearic Islands and for the first time since arriving in the Mediterranean Rosenbaum felt safe.

U-73, a Type VIIB of Admiral Dönitz's 29th Flotilla, first commissioned by Rosenbaum at Bremen in September 1940, had achieved considerable success in her early patrols in the North Atlantic, sinking six British merchant ships totalling 35,171 tons gross, and earning for her commander the Iron Cross First Class. It was an auspicious start to Rosenbaum's career in command.

On her sixth war patrol, *U-73* had been ordered into the Mediterranean to join the 29th Flotilla based at La Spezia, in northern Italy. For Helmut Rosenbaum and his war-weary crew this offered the prospect of a welcome break from the rigours of the grey Atlantic. Unfortunately, 'Mussolini's Lake' at first failed to live up to expectations.

Slipping undetected through the heavily defended Straits of Gibraltar under the cover of darkness on 14 January 1942, Rosenbaum moved to the north-east, hugging the coasts of Spain and France, searching for likely targets. His search was in vain as there appeared to be a dearth of shipping in the area. With the exception of the occasional fishing boat, nothing appeared that would warrant the use of a torpedo. *U-73* reached her new Italian base on 12 February, by which time Rosenbaum had learned that the clear, shallow waters of the Mediterranean were no place for a U-boat to linger. Air patrols by radar-equipped British aircraft were a constant hazard during the daylight hours, a submarine at periscope depth being easily visible from the air. At night, this menace was replaced by the probing Asdic of the enemy's destroyers.

U-73 spent a full month at La Spezia, not embarking on her first Mediterranean war patrol until 16 March 1942, and this patrol was cut short six days later when she was caught on the surface 50 miles off the coast of Libya by a Blenheim of 203 Squadron RAF. The twin-engined fighter/bomber roared in low over the water unseen by *U-73*'s lookouts until it was too late too crash-dive. The U-boat was straddled by four 250lb anti-submarine bombs and was so badly damaged that she was unable to submerge. Fortunately for Rosenbaum, the Blenheim failed to press home her attack and he was able to limp back to La Spezia on the surface, arriving four days later.

Despite being an established Italian naval base repair facilities at La Spezia were indifferent, and four months passed before *U-73* was able to return to sea again. When she did finally sail on 4 August, it soon became evident that the Italian dockyard had done more damage than good. Rather than face another long spell in port, Rosenbaum decided to use his own engineers to carry out the repairs at sea, but within a few hours of sailing it became evident that La Spezia had bestowed another legacy on *U-73*. Helmut Rosenbaum and several of his crew went down with severe stomach pains, indicating possible food poisoning. Some forty-eight hours later, the following entry was made in *U-73*'s log:

> A total of about 1/3 of the crew has come down with fever and diarrhoea. Slow improvement from Castor Oil and milk diet and/or Quinine. As much of the time was spent at periscope depth in warm water, conditions in the boat were rapidly becoming unbearable.

When, during the morning of 7 August, *U-73* reached her appointed station south of the Balearics, her log read:

> With today's weather – completely flat, misty horizon, strong sun, to guarantee remaining unseen the disadvantage of prolonged underwater stays must be accepted.

Despite the unfavourable conditions on board, *U-73*'s patrol continued, as she was now part of an ambush being set up in

response to a report from German agents in Spain that a very
large Allied convoy had left Gibraltar eastbound. Eighteen Italian
and two German submarines, including *U-73*, were lying in wait
between Algiers and the Balearics, while another group of eleven,
again mainly Italian, were deployed between Cape Bon and Sicily.
As a 'backstop' a single Italian submarine was patrolling to the
west of Malta. German Intelligence had conluded that the large
and now known to be heavily escorted convoy was a last-ditch
attempt by the Allies to raise the siege of Malta.

As the Mediterranean summer neared its height, Allied forces
in North Africa were on the retreat. Rommel's tanks were only
35 miles from Alexandria and the Suez Canal was under threat.
However, Rommel's rapid advance had begun to slow, this
being mainly due to the constant attacks on his seaborne convoys by British aircraft and submarines based on the island of
Malta. The island, in turn, was being blockaded and attacked
by the Italian fleet and German and Italian bombers. Malta's
stocks of fuel, ammunition and food were fast running out, and
plans were being laid to mount another major effort to break
through by sea with two convoys simultaneously, one from
Gibraltar in the west and one from Alexandria in the east.

Code-named Operation VIGOROUS, the westbound convoy sailed from Alexandria on 11 June, and consisted of 11 merchant ships escorted by 8 light cruisers, 26 destroyers, 4 corvettes,
2 minesweepers, 9 submarines and 2 rescue ships. Twenty-four
hours later, Operation HARPOON, comprising 6 merchantmen with an escort of one battleship, 2 aircraft carriers, an
anti-aircraft cruiser, 3 light cruisers, 17 destroyers, a minelayer,
4 minesweepers and 6 MTBs, was to leave Gibraltar, eastbound.

British High Command was of the opinion that the twin operation, with its unprecedented show of strength, could not fail
to breach the Axis blockade of Malta, and they probably would
have been right had it not been for a failure of intelligence.
Details of the proposed operations were inadvertently leaked
by the US Military Attaché in Egypt, with disastrous results.
The westbound convoy was ambushed by heavy units of the
Italian Fleet and forced to beat a hasty retreat back to Alexandria.
The HARPOON convoy, meanwhile, despite its big guns and
carrier-borne aircraft, was subjected to continuous attacks by
German and Italian aircraft. Four merchantmen were sunk and

their cargoes lost, the Navy sacrificing a cruiser, five destroyers and an MTB in their defence. The loss of life involved in this fiasco amounted to 301 men, while another 216 were taken prisoner by the enemy.

With the help of fighter cover from Malta in the latter stages of Operation HARPOON, the two merchantmen still afloat reached the beleaguered island with 13,000 tons of supplies, but this was not nearly enough. In July, Lord Gort, Governor of Malta, said that the island had just ten days left before surrender would be unavoidable. General Viscount Alanbrooke, Chief of the Imperial General Staff, after a tour of inspection in early August, wrote:

> The conditions in Malta at that time were particularly depressing, to put it mildly. Shortage of rations, shortage of petrol, a hungry population that rubbed their tummies looking at Gort as he went by, destruction and ruin of docks, loss of convoys just as they approached the island, and the continuing possibility of an attack . . . . without much hope of help or reinforcements . . . . The destruction is inconceivable and reminds me of Ypres, Arras, Lens at their worst during the last war.

Confident that Malta must soon fall into Axis hands, the Luftwaffe had moved some 2,000 fighters and bombers from the Russian Front to bases in Sardinia, South Italy and Sicily, and the island fortress was being bombed day and night with renewed ferocity. The RAF, with too few aircraft, was doing its best to defend the island, but outnumbered ten to one the British pilots were fighting a losing battle. It seemed that surrender, and all this would mean to British troops fighting in the Western Desert, must soon be the only alternative. In desperation, Winston Churchill ordered that yet another attempt be made to run the Axis blockade of the island.

Operation PEDESTAL began on 2 August 1942, when Convoy WS (Winston Special) 21 sailed from the Firth of Clyde with the following ships, many of which had been this way before: Blue Funnel's *Deucalion*, Blue Star Line's *Brisbane Star* and *Melbourne Star*, Clan Line's *Clan Ferguson*, Federal Line's *Dorset*, Glen Line's *Glenorchy*, Port Line's *Port Chalmers* and Shaw Savill's *Empire Hope*, *Waimarama* and *Wairangi*. With them were three

US merchantmen, Grace Line's *Santa Elisa*, Lykes Line's *Almeria Lykes* and Texas Oil Company's tanker, *Ohio*. The last named was on loan to the Ministry of War Transport, and sailed under the British flag with a full British crew. Between them these fourteen ships carried 85,000 tons of supplies, a mix of food, ammunition, fuel and spares, all distributed in such a way that even if only one ship got through to Malta, the island might be able to hold out until more help came.

Escorting WS 21 and determined to defend it to the end, was a British fleet the like of which had rarely been seen at sea since the First World War. Under the overall command of Vice Admiral E. N. Syfret were the battleships *Nelson* and *Rodney*, the aircraft carriers *Eagle*, *Furious*, *Indomitable* and *Victorious*, the anti-aircraft cruiser *Cairo*, the light cruisers *Charybdis*, *Kenya*, *Manchester*, *Nigeria*, *Phoebe and Sirius*. In close support were 33 destroyers, 4 corvettes, 4 minesweepers, 7 fast motor launches and 2 tugs. Vice Admiral Syfret flew his flag in the battleship *Nelson*, and the convoy commodore, Commander A. G. Venables, sailed in the *Port Chalmers*.

During the night of 11/12 August, after four days and nights of aimless patrolling south of the Balearics, Helmut Rosenbaum received a radio signal informing him that a convoy of thirty-six Allied ships had passed through the Straits of Gibraltar and was heading east, presumably bound for Malta. Rosenbaum waited in the convoy's path throughout the night and took *U-73* down to periscope depth at first light on the 12th. For the next six hours, bleary-eyed after yet another sleepless night, he continued to watch and wait. Then shortly before noon, a forest of masts and funnels began to emerge from the haze on the western horizon.

Catching his breath, Rosenbaum adjusted the focus of his periscope and, as the haze thinned, he was able to see what appeared to be a large convoy heading east; eight to ten merchant ships escorted by two cruisers, eight destroyers and three motor launches. He altered course to put the convoy ahead and increased speed.

Half an hour later and the high-sided silhouette of an aircraft carrier was visible bringing up the rear of the convoy. This was the unmissable target he had been waiting for. Rosenbaum sent his crew to their action stations. Creeping closer to the convoy, now definitely confirmed as the enemy, he manoeuvred deftly between the destroyer screen. Some of the heavily loaded merchantmen were crossing his bows no more than 300 metres off, and he was tempted to fire at random and beat a quick retreat, but he was after bigger fish. At last, the aircraft carrier moved across his sights and he gave the order to fire. One after the other, in quick succession, four torpedoes leapt from the bow tubes and sped towards their target.

Stoker Jack Martin, serving in one of HMS *Eagle*'s escorting destroyers, was an eye-witness to what happened next:

> On the Pedestal convoy I happened to be on the upper deck when the *Eagle* was torpedoed. Lots of us saw the whole thing, heard the bangs, saw the ship on one side and then disappear, all in about eight minutes. Something spectacular to watch but awful to realise the large numbers of Navy lads losing their lives or being maimed.

Having fired the opening shot in the running battle of Operation PEDESTAL, Helmut Rosenbaum took *U-73* deep and retired at full speed, with the depth charges of the defending British destroyers raining down in her wake.

HMS *Eagle* capsized and sank in less than eight minutes, leaving behind her a sea of debris and oil in which those who had survived struggled to stay afloat. Thanks largely to the prompt action taken by the destroyers *Laforey* and *Lookout*, 900 of *Eagle*'s total complement of 1,160 were saved, including her commander Captain L. D. Mackintosh.

The attack from the air began in earnest later that day when more than 100 German and Italian high-level and torpedo bombers swooped on the convoy. Sam Peffer, a DEMS gunner serving in the merchantman *Dorset* remembers:

> Every ship was on full alert, expecting to hear the drone of aircraft. In a few hours it would be dusk, the most vulnerable time for the ships. The sun began to sink, a huge ball of red slowly descending towards the sea. Then they came . . . little shapes in the distance . . . . All hell broke loose as they began to dive and the ships began their firing. The noise was deafening, the guns pounding, the roaring of engines and torpedoes exploding. Worst of all was the scream of the Stukas diving.

Shaw Savill's 12,668-ton motor vessel *Empire Hope,* under the command of Captain G. Williams, was first to feel the wrath of the enemy bombers. At about 2100 hrs, she was singled out by a horde of Stukas and subjected to eighteen near-misses, before receiving a direct hit that penetrated her deck before exploding. Loaded as she was with ammunition and aviation spirit, she burst into flame. Able Seaman Bill Cheetham in the destroyer *Bramham* saw her go:

> We were just off Sicily and everything the enemy had was sent to try and get us. We were in a very precarious position because the fires from the other ships lit up the place like daylight.
>
> We steamed towards one of the crippled ships, the s.s. *Empire Hope* and we saw some of her crew struggling in the water and others were in the boats.
>
> Lifeless and mutilated objects that had once been men floated past on both sides and our bows struck two corpses as we steamed forward to assist the remaining survivors.
>
> Some of our crew shouted to them to hurry up as we all had the jitters by now and wanted to feel some speed under us . . . .

Next in line for attack after the *Empire Hope* was Blue Funnel's *Deucalion.* She came in for the full attention of a flight of Ju 88s, and was straddled by a stick of bombs falling so close that several of her hull plates were buckled and the sea poured into her cargo holds. Captain Ramsey Brown pulled his ship out of line and she fell astern, listing heavily. Escorted by HMS *Bramham,* the *Deucalion* limped slowly towards the North African shore, but she made an easy target for an Italian torpedo bomber which roared in low over the water to finish her off. The *Deucalion* also carried thousands of tons of cased petrol and ammunition, and her end was just as sudden and catastrophic as those that had gone before.

The enemy planes, their bomb racks empty, withdrew with the coming of darkness, but any respite for the ships was brief. Soon after midnight, when the convoy was abeam of Cape Bon and entering the narrow channel between the island of Pantelleria and the Tunisian coast, the attack was taken up by

German and Italian E-boats. The following hours, until dawn broke on the 13th, were an absolute nightmare, the fast torpedo boats creating mayhem as they darted in and out of the faltering ranks of the convoy. Their first victim was the cruiser *Manchester*, her hull ripped open by a torpedo, left to sink as the convoy raced on for the safety of Malta.

Having dealt with the main opposition, the E-boats turned their attention to the merchant ships, the Italian boat MS 31 stopping the motor vessel *Glenorchy* with two well-aimed torpedoes. The 8,982-ton liner, with a full deck cargo of aviation spirit in cans, went up like a torch. She sank with the loss of seven of her crew. The remaining eighty-eight men took to the boats, and were taken prisoner when they reached the shore.

There followed a brief lull. Then at about 0300 hrs a second wave of E-boats came barrelling in at full speed, and Shaw Savill's *Wairangi* was hit. Having a similar deck cargo to the *Glenorchy*, she also caught fire and sank. She was followed in the dark hour before the dawn by the American freighter *Almeria Lykes*, torpedoed in her No.1 hold, and abandoned on fire and sinking by her crew. The Italian E-boats then singled out another American, Grace Line's *Santa Elisa*, torpedoing her at close range. She also had aviation spirit on deck, which caught fire and consumed her.

The E-boats withdrew at dawn, to be replaced by a flight of Ju 88 bombers, three of which flew low in line astern to attack the *Clan Ferguson*. The Clan liner's gunners put up such a fierce curtain of fire that the attack became a suicide mission, the leading Junkers being blasted out of the sky, but not before she released her bombs, which were all direct hits. The *Clan Ferguson*, loaded to the gunwales with ammunition and spirit, erupted in sheets of flame and burning debris which, as if in spite, engulfed the other two German planes as they followed in.

An eye-witness on the bridge of the *Waimarama*, which was in an adjacent column directly astern of the *Clan Ferguson* in an adjacent column, reported:

> We hauled out of line after this. I saw a terrible burst of flame half a mile high shoot up into the air. I cannot imagine how any of her crew escaped, but soon after we heard shouts in the water. We could not risk the ship

going too near the flames and were obliged to proceed.
I did not see any escort standing by her so do not think
there could have been any survivors from her. We continued at full speed keeping inside territorial waters
to avoid mines laid outside. For a long time the *Clan
Ferguson* could be seen burning furiously and we saw several ships silhouetted by the light from her.

Second Officer A. M. Black was closer to the action:

I could see flames coming up from the engine room skylight and the ship's side. The hatch covers were blown
off Number Four hold and two landing craft stowed
on top were also blown off. Of the ship's four lifeboats,
Number Three boat was destroyed and all the others
except Number One boat caught fire. Three rafts were
got away. There was a violent explosion in Number Five
hold and the ship appeared to sink about seven minutes
after being hit. The oil blazed on the water for forty-eight
hours and petrol cans kept floating to the surface and
catching fire, as did the oil, causing thick black smoke.
In all sixty-four men got away and were eventually
equally divided on the four rafts, which drifted apart.

In fact the *Clan Ferguson* remained afloat for nearly three hours.
She might have still been saved, had she not been sighted by the
Italian submarine *Bronzo*. Stopped and drifting, the British ship
was an easy target, and the Italian closed in to deliver the *coup
de grâce*. Only a single torpedo was needed to send the burning hulk to the bottom. Ten of her crew were already dead; the
rest escaped in the one remaining lifeboat and four rafts. They
were taken prisoner by the Germans and later handed over to
the Vichy French in Tunisia.

Having narrowly avoided running into the burning *Clan
Ferguson*, the *Waimarama* herself became a target for the Axis
bombers. Captain David MacFarlane in the *Melbourne Star*, following close in the wake of the *Waimarama*, wrote in his report of
the battle:

At 08.10 a.m. 13 August 1942 a covey of dive bombers
suddenly came screaming out of the sun and a stick of
bombs fell on and around the *Waimarama* which blew up

with a roar and a sheet of flame with clouds of billowing smoke, to disappear in a few seconds.

We were showered with debris from this ship, a piece of plating five feet long fell on board. The base of a steel ventilator half an inch thick and 2½ feet high which partly demolished one of our machine-gun posts, a piece of angle iron at the same time narrowly missing a cadet. The sea was one sheet of fire, and as we were so close we had to steam through it. I put the helm hard to port and had to come down from where I was on the monkey island to the bridge to save myself from being burnt. It seemed as though we had been enveloped in smoke and flames for hours, although it was only minutes, otherwise the ship could not have survived. The flames were leaping mast-high, indeed, air pilots reported that at times they reached 2,000 feet.

The heat was terrific. The air was becoming drier every minute, as though the oxygen was being sucked out of it, as in fact it was. When we inspected the damage afterwards we found that nearly all the paint on the ship's side had been burnt away and the bottoms of the liferafts reduced to charcoal.

Such was the confusion of the moment that it seemed that the *Melbourne Star* herself had been hit, so that about thirty-six of her crew, fearing their ship was about to blow up, jumped overboard into the blazing sea. Fourteen of them lost their lives, twenty-two others being rescued by the destroyer *Ledbury*, which despite the smoke and flames steamed into the inferno and picked up another forty-four from both ships.

The convoy was now off the island of Lampedusa and less than 120 miles from Malta. Eight of the merchantmen and their cargoes had been lost, but the one ship whose cargo could spell life or death for the garrison of Malta, the borrowed American oil tanker *Ohio*, was still afloat and under way.

The *Ohio*, commanded by Captain Dudley Mason, with a full British crew, and carrying 11,500 tons of diesel oil and kerosene, had been under almost continuous air attack, but she had the power to hit back. In anticipation of a tough passage, she carried, in addition to the usual merchant ship's armament, a

40mm quick-firing Bofors and six 20mm Oerlikons manned by highly experienced DEMS gunners. German and Italian bombers approaching within range had been given a very hot reception. The tanker had been near-missed by two parachute mines, and two German bombers had crashed on her decks, but she had kept going. It was not until she was attacked by the Italian submarine *Axum* that she faltered.

The *Axum*, under *Commandante* Renato Ferrini, had been stationed 25 miles north-west of Cape Blanc with *U-73* and the others, lying in ambush for the Malta-bound convoy. She had missed the convoy then and Ferrini had moved closer to the Tunisian coast seeking contact. Nothing had been seen until it was dark, and then the flash of gunfire was visible to the north, where the German and Italian bombers were making their final assault on WS 21 before returning to their bases.

Remaining at periscope depth, Ferrini closed the range to about 4,000 yards, where the individual ships were just visible in the dying light. Approaching the outskirts of the convoy, he set his sights on the light cruiser HMS *Nigeria*, which was apart from the other ships. Creeping closer until he was within about 200 yards of the cruiser, Ferrini fired a spread of four torpedoes from his bow tubes.

The torpedoes were well aimed, one hitting the *Nigeria* squarely in her engine room, two dealing a heavy blow to the convoy's air defence by disabling the anti-aircraft cruiser *Cairo*, while the fourth found what was probably the key element in WS 21, the oil tanker *Ohio*.

The *Nigeria*'s engine and boiler rooms were flooded, and she came to a halt with fifty-two of her crew trapped below decks. Those who were able worked frantically to correct the heavy port list the cruiser had acquired and restart the engines. They eventually succeeded with both and, escorted by three destroyers, the *Nigeria* limped back to Gibraltar, where she would spend the next twelve months under repair. HMS *Cairo* fared less well. Her stern was blown clean off and it was soon clear that she would play no further part in the action. She was eventually sunk by gunfire from the destroyer *Derwent*.

As for the tanker *Ohio*, hit by Renato Ferrini's fourth torpedo, she was brought to a standstill with her steering gear out of action and oil spilling out of her ruptured tanks. Fire broke out on deck and there was a move to abandon ship, but Captain Dudley Mason's cool judgement prevailed. Under his direction, hoses were brought to bear on the flames, while the ship's engineers tackled the broken steering gear.

While these heroic efforts were being made to save the *Ohio*, she came under renewed attack from the air. The guns were again manned and, as the light began to fade, Mason and his men fought a running battle with the fires threatening to consume their ship and an enemy intent on inflicting yet more damage.

Mercifully, with the coming of darkness, the bombers withdrew, leaving the *Ohio*'s crew to subdue the flames during the night. By first light next day the fires had been brought under control, and by the time the sun was up the smoke-blackened tanker, with much of her precious cargo still intact, was under way again. She rejoined the convoy and was soon making 16 knots towards Malta, then only 170 miles away – but the fight was not over yet.

Less than an hour after sunrise, the Axis bombers were back, and the assault on the battered *Ohio* resumed. With the help of the destroyers *Ledbury* and *Penn* steaming close on either side, the *Ohio* fought on, repelling the attacks of the enemy with renewed determination. Hit time and time again, she was soon drifting dead in the water, her steering gear smashed beyond repair, her fuel pumps out of action, and more fires breaking out on deck.

It was time for a decision to be made, to abandon the *Ohio*, or make one last attempt to make port. Captain Mason consulted with the Escort Commander and it was decided the tanker was still worth saving. With two destroyers tied up alongside her, HMS *Penn* to port and HMS *Bramham* to starboard, to act as her engines, and the minesweeper *Rye* towing astern to provide steering, the *Ohio* struggled on towards her goal. And that was how, two days later, the battered tanker, harried by enemy bombers to the last, reached the sanctuary of Malta's Grand Harbour with much of her cargo of precious oil still intact.

In this epic battle to relieve Malta, nine of the fourteen fast cargo liners involved were lost, namely *Clan Ferguson, Deucalion, Dorset, Glenorchy, Empire Hope, Waimarama* and *Wairangi,* and the US flag *Almeria Lykes* and *Santa Elisa.* The five that did reach Malta, the *Brisbane Star, Melbourne Star, Port Chalmers, Rochester*

Castle and, last ship in, the tanker *Ohio* were all extensively damaged, but the cargoes they delivered were sufficient to put Malta back on its feet.

Operation PEDESTAL's massive escort force suffered grievously too, losing the aircraft carrier *Eagle*, two cruisers, one of which was the battle-hardened *Cairo*, and one destroyer. Another carrier, a cruiser and a destroyer were seriously damaged.

The human cost of PEDESTAL, forever known on Malta as the Santa Maria Convoy, was equally heavy, the Royal Navy losing 426 men, while the merchant ships lost 120, of whom 83 died in the *Waimarama* conflagration.

CHAPTER THIRTEEN

Dangerous Waters, Dangerous Times

In her heyday, at the height of the First World War, the *City of Cairo* had been a gauntlet runner of some repute, capable of meeting any danger head-on, but the passing years had taken their toll. Now, in the midst of another war, she was sailing in dangerous waters in dangerous times and still running the gauntlet alone.

Registered in Liverpool and owned by Ellerman Lines of London, the *City of Cairo* was a cargo/passenger liner of 8,034 tons, with a declared speed of 12 knots. When she sailed from Bombay in October 1942, she was in her twenty-eighth year and a proven veteran of the UK–South Africa–India trade. Commanded by 46-year-old Captain William Rogerson, she carried British officers and Indian ratings, as was the custom of the trade. In addition, she carried ten DEMS gunners, who serviced her armament consisting of a 12-pounder mounted aft, two 20mm Oerlikons, two twin-Marlin and two twin Hotchkiss machine-guns, and four PAC anti-aircraft rockets. Also on board were 101 passengers, comprising a replacement Lascar crew for another Ellerman ship in Liverpool and a number of civilians, including women and children. The total complement on board on sailing was recorded as 311 persons.

The *City of Cairo*'s cargo consisted of 7,422 tons of Indian produce, namely pig iron, timber, wool, cotton and manganese ore. The last of the bales of cotton was being swung aboard in Bombay when a heavily armed convoy of Army vehicles came alongside and 2,000 boxes, said to contain 100 tons of silver rupees, were loaded into her bullion locker in No. 4 hatch.

First port of call after Bombay was Durban, where the *City of Cairo* was to take on bunkers. It was the change of the monsoon, the Indian Ocean being largely quiescent, and the shortest and quickest route to Durban was via the Mozambique Channel, a passage of some fourteen and a half days. However, it was also the cyclone season in the Indian Ocean, and the prospect of being caught by a cyclone in the Mozambique Channel did not appeal to Captain Rogerson. Furthermore, he had been warned before leaving Bombay that a small group of German long-range U-boats was known to be operating in those waters. Rogerson therefore chose the longer route, passing to the east of Madagascar. His caution was rewarded by an untroubled passage in fair weather, cyclones and the enemy conspicuous by their absence.

Coaling at the Bluff in Durban, then still carried out by hand, was not a pleasant experience, resulting in the ship being covered in a film of coal dust that penetrated deep into the accommodation, even into the food in the galley. When, after twenty-four hours of purgatory, the time came to cast off and return to sea there were few regrets voiced.

Keeping well off the coast to take advantage of the west-going Agulhas Current, the *City of Cairo* made a record passage, dropping anchor in Table Bay on the evening of 30 October. It was spring in the Cape, warm and dry with a fresh sea breeze. As for the war, it might as well have been happening on another planet. There were plenty of uniforms in evidence, but the shops were full, the lights shone brightly at night, and the hospitality shown to visiting seamen by the locals was, as always, legendary.

Stores taken on, fresh water replenished and all formalities completed, the *City of Cairo* sailed from Table Bay at 0600 hrs on the morning of 1 November. When, having cleared South African waters, Captain Rogerson opened his sealed orders he gasped at their contents. The route he was to follow, as laid down by the Admiralty, involved hugging the coast of South Africa for some 800 miles, then crossing the South Atlantic to a position off Brazil in the region of Pernambuco, from whence, under the protection of the US Navy, the *City of Cairo* was to head north to Halifax, Nova Scotia. There she would wait to join a UK-bound transatlantic convoy.

Rogerson scratched his head at the complications that had been added to what was usually a very straightforward 6,000-mile run north, and reached for his charts. He found that the Admiralty route would involve steaming an extra 9,000 miles, adding ten days to the passage, plus any other time spent waiting for convoys to assemble. The risks involved in spending so much extra time exposed to the mercy of the U-boats did not bear thinking about. But the Admirals had spoken and he was in no position to argue.

Zig-zagging by day, and maintaining a straight course at night as instructed, the *City of Cairo* made her way north in favourable weather. No other ships were sighted and, with the exception of the lone albatross that followed in her wake, she appeared to have the ocean to herself. Which was perhaps just as well, for the coal taken on at Durban was proving as dirty as Chief Engineer Bert Sheldon had anticipated. The column of black smoke reaching skywards from the *City of Cairo*'s tall funnel must have been visible over the horizon for many miles around.

Noon sights taken on the 6th put the ship 45 miles abeam of Walvis Bay, in position 23° 30' S 05° 30' W. It was time to alter course. Captain Rogerson made one last sweep of the horizon with his binoculars and gave the order to bring the ship around on to a north-westerly course to pass close south of St. Helena, and so across to a position off the Brazilian coast near Pernambuco. The fine weather was holding, with a light north-westerly breeze and good visibility and, as yet, Rogerson had received no reports of any enemy U-boats or surface raiders being seen in the area. Given a day or two and the south-east trades would be blowing fresh from astern, giving them a helping hand. The portents for a quick uninterrupted passage to the other side of the Atlantic were looking good.

It was not to be. Some 15 miles to the west, and hidden below the horizon, *U-68* was hove to on the surface, lying in wait for whatever might come her way. In her conning tower, *Korvettenkapitän* Karl-Friedrich Merten was also contemplating the future while he searched the empty horizon.

U-68, a Type IXC long-range boat, commissioned by Merten in February 1941, was on her fifth war patrol, having sailed from Lorient in late August to join the newly-formed *Eisbär* Group, a flotilla of five IXCs sent south to seek out Alllied ships off the Cape of Good Hope. *U-68*'s previous record was commendable, having sunk 26 merchantmen totalling 162,117 tons, mainly in the North Atlantic and Caribbean Sea.

Merten's phenomenal good luck had appeared to change when *U-68* joined *Eisbär* in early October 1942, and to date she had sunk just two Allied ships, the Belgian-flag *Belgian Fighter* of 5,403-tons and the US freighter *Examelia* of 4,981 tons, both in the approaches to Cape Town. Since then, in spite of many long hours spent combing the area, she had not sighted a single Allied ship, the usual steady flow of shipping around the Cape having dried up – or so it seemed. On 6 November she had been at sea for 109 days and Merten had received orders to terminate the patrol and return to base.

Despite his recall, Merten had decided to make one last sweep around before setting course for home. The sun went down and darkness closed in, but it was a fine, clear night, and despite the absence of the moon, the thin line of the horizon was still visible. About three hours into the night, what appeared to be a dark cloud was sighted in the east. At first, Merten was inclined to dismiss it as a rain cloud, a line squall perhaps, or was it the smoke rolling back from a ship's funnel? He decided to investigate.

Half an hour passed with only the muffled beat of *U-68*'s twin diesels to disturb the silence of the night, and then the true nature of the 'cloud' was revealed. It was, as Merton had begun to suspect, a pall of smoke beneath which could be seen the blurred outline of a large merchant ship, two masts, tall funnel, high bridge, two well decks. She was steering a north-westerly course at an estimated 12 knots and showing no lights. Evidently British. Going to periscope depth, Merton closed in.

Twenty-four-year-old Third Officer James Whyte had just taken over the watch on the *City of Cairo*'s bridge and was in the chartroom familiarizing himself with the chart. Consequently, he neither heard the strangled cry of the lookout, nor saw the torpedo streaking towards the ship out of the darkness to starboard. It struck just abaft the mainmast, exploding with a roar like a clap of thunder, and blowing a great jagged hole in the ship's plates. The watertight bulkhead between Nos 4 and 5 holds collapsed under the pressure of sea pouring into her hull, and the propeller shaft that ran the length of the two holds was snapped like a twig. The *City of Cairo* drifted to a halt and began to settle quickly by the stern. Assessing the situation as hopeless, Captain Rogerson instructed the radio room to send out a distress call, and gave the order to abandon ship.

The *City of Cairo* carried a total of eight full size lifeboats, one jolly boat and four liferafts, more than enough to accommodate all on board. Angus MacDonald recalled:

> I was a quartermaster and had charge of No.4 lifeboat. After seeing everything in order there, I went over to the starboard side of the ship to where my mate Quartermaster Bob Ironside was having difficulty in lowering his boat. I climbed inside the boat to clear a rope fouling the lowering gear, and was standing in the boat pushing it clear of the ship's side as it was being lowered, when a second torpedo exploded right underneath, and blew the boat to bits. I remember a great flash, and then felt myself flying through space, then going down and down. When I came to I was floating in the water, and could see all sorts of wreckage around me in the dark. I could not get the light on my lifejacket to work, so I swam towards the largest bit of wreckage I could see in the darkness. This turned out to be No.1 lifeboat and it was nearly submerged, it having been damaged by the second explosion. There were a few people clinging to the gunwale, which was down to water level, and other people were sitting inside the flooded boat.
>
> I climbed on board and had a good look around to see if the boat was badly damaged. Some of the gear had floated away, and what was left was in a tangled mess. There were a few Lascars, several women and children and two European male passengers in the boat, and I explained to them that if some of them would go overboard and hang on to the gunwale or the wreckage near us for a few minutes we could bale out the boat and make it seaworthy. The women who were there acted immediately. They climbed outboard, and supported by the lifejackets everyone was wearing, held on to an empty tank that was floating near by. I felt very proud of these women and children. One woman (whose name, if I remember rightly, was Lady Tibbs) had three children and the four of them were the first to swim to the tank. One young woman was left in the boat with two babies in her arms.

We men then started to bale out the water. It was a long and arduous task, as just when we had the gunwale a few inches clear, the slight swell running would roll in and swamp the boat again. Eventually we managed to bale out the boat, and then we started to pick up survivors who were floating on rafts or just swimming. As we worked we could see the *City of Cairo* still afloat, but well down in the water, until we heard someone say, 'There she goes.' We watched her go down, stern first, her bow up in the air, and then she went down and disappeared. There was no show of emotion, and we were all quiet. I expect the others, like myself, were wondering what would happen to us.

We picked up more survivors as the night wore on, and by the first light of dawn the boat was full. There were still people on the rafts we could see with the daylight, and in the distance were other lifeboats. We rowed about, picking up more people, among them Mr. Sydney Britt, and Quartermaster Bob Ironside, who was in No.3 boat with me when the second torpedo struck. Bob's back had been injured, and one of his hands had been cut rather badly. We picked up others, then rowed to the other boats to see what decision had been made about our future. Mr. Britt had, naturally, taken over command of our boat, and now he had a conference with Captain Rogerson, who was in another boat. They decided we would make for the nearest land, the island of St. Helena, lying 500 miles due north. We transferred people from boat to boat so that families could be together. Mr. Britt suggested that, as our boat was in a bad way, with many leaks and a damaged rudder, and at least half its water supply lost, all the children should shift to a dry boat and a few adults should take their places in our boat. When everything was settled we set sail on our long voyage . . . .

The decision to head for St. Helena had not been an easy one to make. Some 800 miles to the east lay the coast of Africa, a tempting and unmissable landfall. But both Rogerson and Britt were experienced navigators and aware that if anyone survived the long sea passage eastwards, which was doubtful, the boats would probably end up being thrown ashore amongst the unin-habited sandhills of Namibia. On the other hand, although the island of St. Helena might be only a tiny speck on the face of this great ocean, its peak was 2,600 feet high, visible on a clear day at 50 miles. Furthermore, if they chose to go north, both the prevailing winds and currents would be behind them. St. Helena it was.

At best, the voyage north to St. Helena would take two or three weeks, and would require careful navigation, for which each of the *City of Cairo*'s lifeboats was equipped with a magnetic compass and a small scale chart of the Atlantic Ocean. In addition, Second Officer Leslie Boundy had rescued his sextant from the sinking ship, and Captain Rogerson had his Rolex watch, which was accurate enough to serve as a chronometer. If the boats were able to keep in sight of one another, and strict rationing of food and water was enforced, their goal was obtainable.

Ship's Writer Jack Edmead wrote the following report in March 1943:

> At daybreak on the 7th November the Captain called a muster; it was found that 3 passengers and a Wireless Operator were missing. I then heard that the 2nd Wireless Operator had transmitted an SOS message and had received an acknowledgement from Cape Town before the ship sank. When it became light I, accompanied by several of the crew, swam to the capsized lifeboats. We succeeded in righting one of these boats, but on bailing it out we found it was leaking badly through one or two of the seams. I cut a hole in my lifejacket, pulled out some kapok, plugging this with some white lead into the seams. Finally, 54 of us managed to get into this lifeboat with the Chief Officer in charge.
>
> During the morning we collected all the food, water and gear from the four rafts, dividing it amongst the other lifeboats. The Captain ordered all the boats to set sail and steer NNE keeping together during the daylight and lying up in line ahead at night. As our boat was still making water it was necessary to maintain 2 hour pumping watches, day and night, to prevent the boat from becoming waterlogged. On the 8th November the Chief Officer asked permission from the Captain to leave the

other boats and proceed to St. Helena as our boat was the fastest sailer. The Captain was reluctant to agree, but on the following day, realizing that our boat could sail a great deal faster than the others, he agreed to let us sail for St. Helena, which was estimated to be about 220 miles distant. The Chief Officer reckoned that we could make this island in about 12 days.

Accordingly, on the evening of the 9th November our boat left the other six and continued independently. There were 54 men in the boat, 11 crew, including a Doctor, a Captain Royal Navy, and one woman. The Chief Officer took charge of the lifeboat, ably assisted by Captain MacCall, Royal Navy, and we sailed through very fine weather with slight seas for about 9 days without incident.

The Chief Officer rationed the food and water, allowing 3 meals a day, each meal consisting of 4oz of water, biscuits, pemmican, chocolate and horlicks tablets. There was plenty of food with more than 30 gallons of water in the lifeboat, and it was estimated that with these rations we could exist for about 3 months. After about the 10th day, as land was not sighted the natives grew very low spirited, becoming unwilling to assist in bailing the boat, consequently the Europeans had to do twice as much work. Some of the natives began to drink salt water this time, which made them more thirsty, and from the 10th day onwards several natives were delirious. From noon until about 1800 each day the sun beat down on us unmercifully and it was impossible to keep cool. An old flag was torn up, each man was given a small piece to put over his head. On the 11th day the first native died, and during the next few days they died two and three at a time. It was about this time that some of the Europeans began to lose heart, several of them dying at various intervals. Death in each case seemed to follow an attack of delirium lasting about 3 hours. From this time onwards the crew gradually lost their appetites and the water situation became very grave. On the 14th day the Chief Officer died, so Captain MacCall R N took charge and carried on with the steering. Some of the men gargled with salt water, while others used a solution of iodine and salt water, but after the 15th day several of them suffered from acute sore throats. One of the quartermasters developed a high fever which lasted for three days before he died; just about this time Captain MacCall died during the 16th day. Three men died on various days until on the 28th day there were only 6 of us left, the water had practically given out and there was only one more ration remaining for each.

The ordeal dragged on for another eight days, with the remaining survivors becoming weaker by the hour, until they were too weak even to bail. The water in the boat rose gradually higher until, on the thirty-sixth day adrift, 12 December, it was washing over the thwarts on which they sat. Others had died one by one, until only Jack Edmead, Quartermaster Angus MacDonald, and a woman passenger were still alive. Then, at long last, came deliverance. Jack Edmead wrote:

At 0830 on the 36th morning – 12th December – I suddenly heard the noise of an engine, which seemed to be very close to the lifeboat. At first I thought it must be an aircraft, but I was too weak to even hoist the red sails, so I burned a flare and shouted loudly. Immediately a voice answered me 'All right.' I then realised slowly that there was a ship very close to us, so I lay back in the lifeboat and waited.

By the most incredible stroke of bad luck, Jack Edmead and his fellow survivors had drifted into the path of the German blockade runner *Rhakotis*, which was hove to with engine failure. They were taken on board the merchant ship, where they received the best treatment the ship's doctor could provide. Unfortunately, the woman was beyond saving, and she died five days later. Jack Edmead and Angus MacDonald were nursed back to health while on board the *Rhakotis*, but their adventure did not end there. On 1 January 1943, the *Rhakotis* was intercepted by the British cruiser HMS *Scylla* while in the Bay of Biscay and sunk, and Edmead and MacDonald found themselves once more having to abandon ship. Jack Edmead was picked up by a Spanish fishing boat and taken into Corruna, and was eventually repatriated to the UK, but Angus MacDonald had the crowning misfortune to be rescued by a U-boat, and spent the rest of the war in a German prisoner-of-war camp.

Of the *City of Cairo's* total complement of 311, only 18 were killed when the torpedo struck. The remaining 86 who lost their lives all died of exposure in the lifeboats, which serves to illustrate how inadequate the 'open boats' of the Second World War were. Chief Officer Britt's boat was the better sailer and, as related by Jack Edmead, had gone on ahead with the intention of landing on St. Helena and bringing help to the others, but unfortunately overshot the island. Just three of the boat's original complement of 54 survived, only to fall into the hands of the enemy.

No.4 boat, the smallest of the eight, in the charge of Third Officer James Whyte, having failed to sight St. Helena after seventeen days, opted to make for the coast of South America, 1,500 miles to the west. After an epic voyage of fifty-one days, only Whyte and a woman passenger were alive when their boat was sighted by the Brazilian Navy's minelayer *Caravelas*. Sadly, James Whyte lost his life when returning across the Atlantic in the *City of Pretoria*, which was torpedoed by *U-172* on 4 March 1943 and was lost with all hands.

The other lifeboats all reached safety with no lives lost. Boats Nos 5, 6 and 7, carrying Captain Rogerson and 154 others, were rescued by passing ships on 19 November, and their occupants landed at St. Helena, while on that same day, No.8 boat, with forty-seven on board, was sighted by the southbound British ship *Bendoran* and landed at Cape Town. Of those rescued alive, one died aboard the *Bendoran*, two died after being picked up by the *Clan Alpine*, and four others died in hospital on St. Helena.

In September 1981, thirty-nine years after the *City of Cairo* was sunk, the *Sunday Express* published the story of the loss of the ship. This prompted a reply from Karl-Friedrich Merten, then in retirement after a post-war career in ship building, an extract from which I give below:

> A statement in your account of the City of Cairo sinking and aftermath I must oppose strongly, namely 'This time his tone was more menacing and the U-boat's guns were trained directly on them'. . . . This was

completely incorrect. *U-68* trained no guns of any kind at any time on those unfortunate shipwrecked people or any others. Survivors were not considered 'enemies' but as tragic human beings with an extremely uncertain fate. To assist them within the framework of orders and security of one's own ship and crew was a seaman's obligation and duty.

Of course, I concede an author's licence to ornament his story a little on minor points, but he has to remain within the truth especially as far as the behaviour of named individuals is concerned. It was, for example, unimportant to narrate that 'closing the lifeboats at periscope depth, Merten surfaced and climbed into the conning tower'. In fact the complete action took place on the surface! At that period there was no possibility whatsoever of attacking a ship on a dark night by periscope in a submerged state.

Your readers may care to know that the three lifeboats controlled by *U-68* were not even half occupied – with nearly all men. Women and children were drifting around crying for help in the water but nobody made any attempt to use the oars to go for those swimming! It needed my loudest shouting by megaphone to create at least the initiative to help those in the water clinging to the outside of the gunwale. So I shouted: 'Care immediately for those swimming!'

Further, I called for the 'City of Cairo's' captain, not to take him prisoner, but to make him responsible for an immediate rescue operation and for a fair distribution of survivors among the existing lifeboats sufficient to give slight hope for survival and providing an officer for navigation. However, the captain remained hidden!

When we received the distress call from the 'City of Cairo' after torpedoing her and we heard about the large number of people on board, we found it difficult to comprehend the irresponsibility of the Allied authorities in sending her out of Capetown without a naval escort, at a time when it was well known to all responsible authorities that a pack of submarines was assembled and in operation around the Cape.

Merten's letter to the *Sunday Express* was quickly answered by
Dr Douglas Quantrill, who had been the *City of Cairo*'s surgeon
at the time:

> As regards the German captain's account of his encoun-
> ter with the 'City of Cairo', he is very unfair indeed.
> Perhaps I can remember the details better than he can.
>
> First we did not expect an enemy submarine to pick
> up over two hundred survivors. Such a procedure
> would have been foolhardy.
>
> As he was not sighted on the surface before he
> approached the lifeboats we assumed he attacked
> from below. If we were wrong is it relevant?
>
> There were more men than women in the boats
> because there were far more men than women involved
> in the whole incident. There were also more men than
> women not in lifeboats after the sinking.
>
> We saw guns in the conning tower, and they appeared
> to be pointing at us. If they were it is not surprising.
> One of us could have had a gun and been brave or
> impetuous enough to use it.
>
> We were ordered to 'stop rowing and keep still' and
> obviously we obeyed and so could not continue to pick
> up survivors while we were being interrogated.
>
> To imply that our Captain was hiding in a lifeboat is
> a wicked accusation. He was sucked under when the
> ship went down and while we were being questioned he
> was well out of earshot, floating about in his lifejacket
> vomiting large quantities of sea water.
>
> It was unfortunate that we were not escorted by the
> Royal Navy but we all accepted that to expect escorts
> for every British ship was quite unrealistic. In 1942 there
> were just not escort ships available.
>
> Finally, I was glad to know that the U-boat captain
> survived the formidable wartime dangers he must
> have encountered. In spite of everything, I shall always
> remember the civilised way in which he dealt with the
> situation and his efforts to help us on our way. I am sur-
> prised that he jumped to such unfair conclusions.

The wreck of the *City of Cairo* lies 2,800 fathoms deep, and was long considered to be beyond the reach of man. And so she would have remained, but the lure of those 2,000 boxes of silver rupees stowed in her No.4 hold was strong. In September 2013, seventy-one years after she succumbed to Karl-Friedrich Merten's torpedoes, the British salvage company Deep Ocean Search sent down a robot which penetrated the ship's strongroom and brought to the surface coins to the value of £34 million.

CHAPTER FOURTEEN

A Sense of Duty

Having served at sea in the First World War, Captain Selwyn Capon knew at once what was in the air when the naval officer with the briefcase was shown into his cabin. His ship was wanted on Admiralty business.

It was November 1941, and Blue Star Line's *Empire Star* was lying in Liverpool ready to load her next outward cargo. Ordinarily, this would have been a variety of manufactured goods destined for various ports in South Africa, Australia and New Zealand, but this was wartime and the rules were changing.

Completed at Harland & Wolff's Belfast yard in December 1935, the *Empire Star* was a 12,656-ton refrigerated motor vessel powered by two 6-cylinder Burmeister & Wain diesel engines driving twin screws and having a service speed of 16 knots. She was manned by a crew of seventy-five under the command of 52-year-old Captain Selwyn Norman Capon, OBE, whose decoration was awarded in the First World War, during which he served as junior officer with Blue Star.

In the winter of 1941 Britain's fortunes were at a low ebb. Things were not going well in the Western Desert, and in the Far East the dark clouds of war were gathering as the Japanese flexed their muscles. British territory in that area was under threat, particularly rubber-rich Malaya, and the garrison of Singapore was in urgent need of reinforcement. Consequently, the *Empire Star*, her holds filled with military stores and equipment, found herself leaving Liverpool with the fast 'Winston Special' convoy, WS 12Z.

WS 12Z sailed from the Mersey on 12 November 1941 and consisted of sixteen fast merchantmen carrying 22,000 troops and their equipment. The heavily escorted convoy sailed south to the Cape and then north to Bombay, on India's west coast, which was reached on 6 January 1942. Meanwhile, the Japanese had landed in Malaya and were already threatening Singapore. The *Empire Star* and four other ships, loaded with 11,665 troops and their equipment, were hastily despatched in convoy from Bombay, but by the time they arrived off Singapore on 29 January, the island fortress was beyond saving. What had started as a rescue mission turned into a race to evacuate as many people from Singapore as possible before the Japanese broke through.

At first light on 12 February the *Empire Star*, requisitioned by the Admiralty, was hustled out of Singapore Roads with her outward cargo still on board and with some 2,160 refugees packed shoulder to shoulder above and below decks. This included in addition to her 75 crew, 1,573 British Army, Navy and RAF personnel, 139 Australian troops, and 133 Australian Army nurses. With the Japanese at the gates of Singapore no one was really counting, so this was a very rough estimate and could be seriously in error either way, but the ship was certainly dangerously overcrowded. In company with the *Empire Star* was the Blue Funnel steamer *Gorgon*, similarly packed with refugees. Escorting the two rescue ships were the First World War vintage light cruiser HMS *Durban*, and HMS *Kedah*, an ex-Singapore-Penang ferry converted for anti-submarine work.

The Japanese were by this time in control of the waters surrounding Singapore, and within three hours of leaving the island the small convoy was under attack from the air. At about 0915 hrs, while the ships were still among the islands in the Durian Strait, six Japanese dive bombers dropped out of the clouds without warning. All ships immediately opened fire with every gun they could bring to bear, and the barrage they put up was so heavy that the bombers were forced to retire, one being shot down and another damaged. The *Empire Star*, being by far the largest of the four ships, came in for the most attention and was hit by three bombs, which killed fourteen and wounded seventeen people on her crowded decks. The ship was set on fire and one of her four lifeboats was damaged. Had it not been for evasive action taken by Captain Capon, who manouvred the ship, assisted by Third Officer James Smith and the Singapore pilot George Wright, who were calling the fall of the shot, the damage might have been far worse. In spite of the mayhem discipline prevailed, and fire parties led by Chief Officer Joseph Dawson tackled the fires, while the Australian nurses looked after the wounded.

That was only the beginning. Japanese high level bombers followed, and throughout the rest of the morning the convoy was subjected to unrelenting attacks. Each time, Captain Capon, with the help of Third Officer Smith and George Wright, took violent evasive action to dodge the bombs, and the *Empire Star* escaped without further damage.

Shortly after noon the bombers gave up and went away, leaving the convoy to press on at all speed. The safe harbour of Batavia, not yet occupied by the Japanese, was reached late on the 13th. The *Empire Star* spent two days in the port under repair, before going on to Fremantle alone, arriving eight days later.

An eye-witness report of the action was later recorded by John R. Gibbs, RAF:

> Soon after we sailed on the 12th February, we were attacked by a formation of Japanese bombers, perhaps the same ones who had so recently sunk the *Prince of Wales*. When the bombing started I went down the nearest hold, which I found was full of vehicles, many obviously with petrol in them. I felt very vulnerable, so each time the noise lessened I attempted to escape up the metal ladder, only to be driven back by a hail of bullets from the planes and the noise of our own machine gun manned by soldiers and mounted on a wooden turret. Eventually after several hours the mayhem ceased, when I looked out of the hold again the machine gun turret had disappeared and presumably the soldiers with it.
>
> The following day was Friday the 13th and we thought surely they would come back and finish us off, but it did not happen. A small service was held and the bodies of those killed in the attack were slid down a shoot [*sic*], covered by a flag, to be buried at sea. We continued on our way to Batavia with no other troubles, other than lack of food and toilet facilities. Due to the skilful action of the Captain in zig zagging and taking avoiding action, the damage to the ship seemed to be remarkably little. One bomb had hit the front end and another had hit the raised cabins in the middle, the top of which had been opened up like a tin can. . . . I consider myself very lucky to have been on the *Empire Star*, and for me Friday the 13th is a lucky day!

In September 1942, a number of awards were made in recognition of the *Empire Star*'s part in the evacuation of Singapore. Captain

Selwyn Capon, who already held the OBE for service in the First World War, was made CBE. Chief Officer Joseph Dawson and Chief Engineer Richard Francis were awarded the OBE, Second Officer James Golightly, Senior Second Engineer Herbert Weller and Third Officer James Smith were awarded the MBE, while Boatswain William Power and Carpenter Sydney Milne were awarded the BEM. Commendations were also awarded to Junior Engineers J. J. Johnson, J. Middleton, and J. R. Mitchhell, Cadets R. Foulkner, and R. Perry, Able Seaman C. P. Barber, Donkeyman H. E. Heaver and Stewards C. E. Ribbons and T. S. Hughes.

The subsequent entry in the *London Gazette* read:

> The Master's coolness, leadership and skill were out-standing and it was mainly due to his handling of the ship that the vessel reached safety.
>
> The Chief Officer showed great organising ability and tireless leadership throughout. Under the direction of the Chief Engineer, the Engineer Officers remained at their posts throughout the attacks and kept the engines and fire service pumps working, thus releasing all others of the engine room staff to help the fire parties. The Second Officer was in charge of the guns and fought them with gallantry throughout the attacks. One aircraft was shot down and one certainly damaged by the combined fire of the ship and her escort.
>
> The Boatswain and Carpenter behaved magnificently throughout. They led the crew and worked tirelessly during the attacks. They were always prominent, lead-ing fire parties, dealing efficiently with fires and led parties that carried the wounded to hospital.

In a letter to Blue Star Line's Head Office Captain Capon wrote:

> Actually we, each one of us on board at the time simply did our duty; what, under circumstances of any such emergency, was commonly expected and required of us. In such circumstances, as I feel sure you will under-stand and appreciate, it is team work which so materi-ally counts and that, in a great measure, accrues from example and leadership born of a high sense of duty.

Thanks to the bravery and devotion to duty of Captain Capon and his crew more than 2,000 British and Australian personnel escaped from Singapore as it fell to the Japanese. The *Empire Star* arrived in Sydney on 4 March, where more permanent repairs were carried out. Having discharged her cargo of military stores she then reverted to her normal service, loading frozen lamb and wool in Australian and New Zealand ports. She then sailed east across the Pacific, crossed into the Atlantic via the Panama Canal, and arrived back in Liverpool on 11 September 1942.

This momentous voyage over, Captain Selwyn Capon commented:

> Of my ship's company, during those particularly hectic days, I can only speak in terms of highest commendation, for, apart from their outstanding coolness in moments of greatest danger, the kindly consideration extended & the help given wherever and whenever needed to both Service personnel & civilian refugees alike under those most distressing circumstances & trying conditions was something typically & truly British & therefore something good to see & to be able to record. This ready disposition on the part of the ordinary merchant sailor revealed itself as a somewhat surprising feature where a great many of those carried during that particular emergency were concerned. They certainly will have good cause to long remember it.
>
> We men of the Merchant Navy grimly carry on despite the heavy balance of odds against us. We are amongst the last to receive any pat on the back, but we foster no heartaches over that fact. We neither look for them nor in any way invite them. Whether it be in normal times of Peace or in having to contend with abnormal circumstances of War, we come & we go, just carrying on getting things done, but with the minimum of publicity & no fuss. Amongst ourselves sufficient it is for us that in our own hearts we have the proud knowledge & the gratification of a job well done; of having done & all through doing what is demanded & expected of us & this to the fullest extent of our ability. . . .

When she sailed from Liverpool some five weeks later, the *Empire Star* was once more loaded down to her marks with military equipment, a cargo of 10,555 tons which included 2,000 bags of mail, ammunition and aircraft on deck. She was bound for Suez via the Cape. As had become the norm, she would sail alone and unescorted. Captain Selwyn Capon was still in command, but Chief Officer Dawson had left the ship, being replaced by Chief Officer Leslie Vernon, and Third Officer Smith had been promoted to Second Officer in the ship, his place being taken by Third Officer Roland Moscrop-Young. Also on board were nineteen passengers, including four women and two children, all civilians returning to South Africa.

Routed well out into the Atlantic to avoid the packs of U-boats haunting the Western Approaches, the *Empire Star* ran into heavy weather within hours of clearing the North Channel. The great ocean was at its equinoctial worst, with a north-westerly wind climbing towards storm force, rough seas, and a mountainous swell coming in from the west. But she was built for this kind of weather, and the *Empire Star* was able to maintain a speed of 14 knots. By the afternoon of 23 October, she was 570 miles north of the Azores and altering south for the Cape. Despite the wind and seas the sky was clearing and visibility was good, giving promise of better weather as they moved south. Captain Capon had received no reports of U-boats on his projected route and was optimistic of an untroubled passage to Cape Town. His optimism was to prove mistaken.

The Type VIIC *U-615*, on her first war patrol, with *Kapitänleutnant* Rolf Kapitzky in command, had sailed from Kristiansand, where she had called for fresh water, on 8 September, bound for her patrol area south of Cape Farewell. The voyage was without incident until she passed south of Iceland. From then on it was as if she had disturbed a veritable hornet's nest of Allied aircraft; every time she came to the surface she was set upon. Fortunately, she was well equipped to deal with the attacks, being armed with two 20mm AA guns mounted abaft the conning tower, and four machine guns, two singles and two twins, in the tower.

On 11 October, after a month of fruitless patrolling in subarctic conditions, *U-615* at last made contact with an enemy ship. She was the 4,221-ton US-owned *El Lago*, sailing under the

Panamanian flag. The *El Lago* had left Reykjavik, bound New York, with Convoy ONS 136, but owing to horrendous weather conditions, described as 'hurricane force winds, tremendous heavy seas, rain and poor visibility', she had been forced to leave the convoy and was alone, hove-to head to wind and sea, just able to maintain steerage way.

Kapitzky submerged and stalked the *El Lago* until darkness fell, then closed in to attack. Remarkably, given the weather, the two torpedoes Kapitzky fired both hit the target, breaking her back. The *El Lago* went down quickly, but not before two life-boats and several rafts were launched. Kapitzky approached the boats and took prisoner both the Master and Chief Engineer of the Panamanian. Out of the *El Lago*'s total complement of fifty-nine they were the only survivors. The others were never seen again.

Encouraged by his first success, Ralph Kapitzky remained in the area and twelve days later sighted the unescorted *Empire Star*. The weather had moderated somewhat, but it was still blowing hard from the north-west, with very rough seas and a heavy swell, and to prevent damage to his unprotected deck cargo of aircraft Captain Capon had ceased to zig-zag. He had not reduced speed, however, and the *Empire Star* was still ploughing through the heavy seas at 14 knots.

On sighting the *Empire Star* Kapitzky submerged, and studied the lone ship for about forty minutes before deciding she was a legitimate target. Satisfied, he manoeuvred into position, and at 1543 hrs fired a full spread of four torpedoes from his bow tubes. The entry in *U-615*'s log reads:

> 18.52 (15.52 local time) 4-fan with fixed angle.
>
> After 61 seconds a bright metallic impact heard in the entire boat, suspect a pistol failure. After 67 seconds hit aft, after 20 seconds another explosion in the ship. Enemy ship is the 'SYDNEY STAR' class.
>
> Ship turns to port and remains stopped on heading 30°, light list to starboard, does not sink, stern lies some-what deeper, on the stern structure a cannon of at least 10.5 cm, unmanned.

Having fought an exhausting three-day battle with the weather and reached 1,000 miles out into the Atlantic, Captain Capon was giving little thought to the other enemy. So concerned was he with the safety of the valuable aircraft lashed down on the *Empire Star*'s hatch-tops that he had not even sent his gunners to man the 4-inch anti-submarine gun, which was customary as dusk approached. Neither he, nor anyone else on the bridge, had seen the U-boat lurking on the surface, nor did they see the wash of her periscope as she manoeuvred for the kill.

The first indication that they were under attack came when the *Empire Star* staggered as she was hit by Rolf Kapitzky's first torpedo, which failed to explode. Seconds latter came the real thing, a roar and a blinding flash as Kapitzky's second torpedo slammed into the engine room on the starboard side. The four men of the watch below were killed by the explosion, two others on the upper platform were injured and, as the sea poured into the engine room, all the lights went out, the engines stopped, and the ship took a sudden lurch to starboard.

There was no immediate panic, though given the horror of the situation this might have been excused, and all surviving crew and passengers mustered on the boat deck. The *Empire Star* carried four lifeboats, but one of the starboard-side boats had been destroyed by the blast of the torpedo. However, there was ample room in the remaining three boats for all on board. When the order to abandon ship was given, despite the heavy list and the high sea and swell running, all boats were launched safely and cleared the ship's side.

As the boats lay hove-to, rolling in the lee of the stricken ship, she slowly came back upright, and there seemed to be a possibility of reboarding her, but *Kapitänleutnant* Kapitzky was not about to let that happen. Remaining submerged, he turned *U-615* short-about and, taking careful aim, delivered what he intended as the *coup de grâce* with his stern tube. The torpedo ran amok and missed completely. Undeterred, Kapitzky reloaded his bow tubes and tried again with a single shot. The torpedo was seen to hit the *Empire Star* amidships, but she stubbornly refused to sink.

Having come this far and failed to sink this British ship with six valuable torpedoes, Kapitzky was near despair, but he persevered. Moving closer, he fired again. This time the result was instantaneous. The *Empire Star* reared her bows high in the air and, two and a half hours after the first torpedo struck, went down stern first in a flurry of smoke and spray. Some minutes after she disappeared, there was a heavy underwater explosion. An entry in *U-615*'s log reads:

> Very heavy explosion, suspect munitions or depth charge self ignition. Also aircraft bomb possible, at periscope depth heavy concussion in the boat, otherwise nothing noted.
>
> Piston sounds to the north, very faint, moved off in an easterly direction.
>
> Surfaced. I run from sinking location with good visibility, nothing more seen, ran off because the ship transmitted to an escort, sinking assured and search for the Captain at night has little prospect of success. . . .

After the *Empire Star* had disappeared below the waves, Captain Capon fully expected the U-boat to surface to interrogate the survivors, which was customary, and in accordance with orders issued by Admiral Dönitz, C-in-C U-boats. Those orders also included taking prisoner, whenever possible, the ship's Master and Chief Engineer, which was part of a policy to create a shortage of trained senior officers in Allied shipping. Aware of this danger, Capon and Chief Engineer Francis had already stripped off their badges of rank and were preparing to hide to avoid that fate. However, Rolf Kapitzky had decided that the possibility of his victim's broadcast SOS attracting an enemy warship and the state of the weather were excuse enough, and *U-615* had already left the scene of the sinking without surfacing.

As soon as it was obvious that the U-boat was no longer around, Chief Officer Vernon searched the area, discovered nine other survivors clinging to five liferafts and took them aboard his already overcrowded boat.

The *Empire Star*'s lifeboats, as befitted a ship of her calibre, were heavy wooden craft built to withstand the worst weather, and each designed to accommodate forty men. But they were open boats, offering little protection from wind and waves, and throughout that night the survivors were tossed around and constantly drenched by the icy spray. By the time the cold light of dawn came, after a night spent fighting to keep the boat's head to wind and sea to avoid being swamped or capsized, the occupants were thoroughly exhausted and demoralized. Chief Officer Vernon later wrote, 'We lay to a sea anchor during the night; but in addition to the sea anchor we had to use five oars to keep the boat's head to sea and avoid flooding. I tried to communicate with the other boats by light; but was unsuccessful.'

Their predicament was dire. Their ship had gone, blown from under them without warning, their SOS had not been acknowledged and there was little hope of rescue. That left them adrift in mid-Atlantic, 600 miles from the nearest land; it was blowing a full gale from the west, gusting to storm force 10, and the boats were rolling their gunwales under, constantly awash from the angry breaking seas. The three boats were each certified to accommodate forty persons, but the Board of Trade's allowance of 9 cubic feet per person was never realistic. In this case, Captain Capon's boat carried thirty-eight, Chief Officer Vernon's boat held thirty-four, and Third Officer Moscrop-Young's twenty-seven. It is on record that all three boats, even the Third Officer's, were all uncomfortably overcrowded. Lesser men would have thrown in the towel there and then.

The primary role of the lifeboat is to get passengers and crew off a sinking ship and keep them afloat until rescue arrives. It is built to withstand heavy weather, but is a cumbersome craft and not easy to handle. Under sail, it has all the characteristics of drunken crab, and stubbornly refuses to go closer than eight points to the wind. Chief Officer Vernon, who wrote a report on the aftermath of the sinking, said, 'If for any reason a boat got beam on to the sea for two or three successive heavy seas I consider that in the conditions prevailing she could easily have capsized.' The only way to make any progress was to run before the wind. With this in mind, Captain Capon decided to head south for the Azores.

On a southerly course, with the wind just abaft the beam, the boats made slow progress, but any attempt to keep together became a farce. Lashed by blinding rain squalls and staggering from crest to trough, they soon separated and lost sight of each other. Chief Officer Vernon's report described how the weather had deteriorated so much by nightfall on the 24th that he was forced to lower the sails and once again stream his sea anchor to avoid broaching to. There followed a thoroughly unpleasant night, in which the boat's rudder was smashed by the seas and a steering oar manned by two men was used to help hold her head into the wind.

After an agonizingly long wait, daylight finally came on the 25th, and Vernon was forced to admit to himself that the situation was hopeless. They were drifting helplessly at the mercy of the wind and waves, without sails, without rudder, staring death in the face. Then the miracle happened. The wind eased, the seas slackened their onslaught, and out of gloom of the storm appeared HMS *Black Swan.*

It so happened that when the *Empire Star* was under attack, the Royal Navy sloop *Black Swan*, commanded by Commander T. A. C. Pakenham, had just left a westbound convoy in mid-Atlantic, and was about to return to Liverpool. She had been close enough to the torpedoed ship to pick up her SOS, and had been searching for survivors ever since. All thirty-four in Chief Officer Vernon's boat were taken on board the sloop, then *Black Swan* carried out a 120-mile-wide search for the other boats. Next morning, Third Officer Moscrop-Young's lifeboat was found, and all twenty-seven on board rescued. The third life-boat was never seen again, and it was concluded that Captain Selwyn Capon and all those with him had perished in the storm.

Some months later, Mr W. A. Smith, who had been a pas-senger in the *Empire Star*, wrote a letter to Blue Star Line:

> I cannot fully enjoy the feeling of safety without mak-ing comments on the behaviour of your officers and men at the recent disaster – Chief Officer Vernon and Second Officer Smith upheld the true traditions of the Merchant Navy. These officers worked with unflinch-ing courage throughout. The boat was handled with skill in fearful weather. Both officers never tired in their fight for our lives. They always had words of encour-agement for their passengers. I would also like to make special mention of Mr. Donaldson A.B. This man worked like a Trojan throughout our ordeal. The excellent radio service on board certainly set the rescue machine in motion, but I feel certain that Messrs. Vernon and Smith were very largely responsible for our salvation. To these fine officers I say thank you, and may God grant them their reward in the trying days ahead of us.

Captain Selwyn Capon, his officers and crew, had most cer-tainly given of their best. On two occasions, in the evacuation of

Singapore and when torpedoed in mid-Atlantic, they had shown exemplary courage and resourcefulness. Forty-four of them, including Captain Capon, had given their lives in the preservation of their ship, its passengers and cargo. Nothing more could be asked of them. As for their Nemesis, *U-615*, she could not have embarked on her first war patrol at a more inopportune time. Allied aircraft had gained control of the skies above the Atlantic, and from the moment she left the safety of the Baltic she had been pounced upon and forced to crash dive with depth bombs exploding around her. This continued throughout her short life, culminating in a prolonged battle with American aircraft in the Caribbean in August 1943. A US Navy report on the interrogation of those who survived the sinking of *U-615* gives the details:

U-615 was in the act of making a routine dive when she was attacked on 6 August 1943 by a PBM from Squadron 204. The attack took place at 1721Z in 12° 38' N, 64° 15' W. Three or four depth charges were dropped and damaged the U-boat considerably. The electric motors and port Diesel were put out of action. The lubricating oil gravity tank was damaged and oil ran into the bilges. High pressure air lines were broken and water entered through some of the glands. The U-boat surfaced at once, and the two 20mm anti-aircraft guns were manned. The portable machine guns were brought to the bridge, and the U-boat opened fire. The plane returned to the attack, but was shot down by the heavy barrage laid down by the 20mm guns.

A second PBM attacked *U-615* at 1935Z, and at 2040Z another PBM and a PV joined in action. These attacks increased the damage aboard the U-boat. During the night of 6–7 August 1943, *U-615* drifted helplessly on the surface. Kapitzky had been wounded severely in the thigh by machine-gun fire and it became clear that he was bleeding to death. The crew gathered on deck awaiting the order to abandon ship. Kapitzky bade farewell to his men. The Executive Officer then gave orders to break out the rubber boat, intending to use it for Kapitzky and a wounded petty officer. In the darkness and confusion, the boat drifted away.

According to one prisoner, the Executive Officer asked for volunteers to swim after the rubber boat, but no one answered the call. He then ordered four men at pistol point to swim for it. They obeyed, but only three returned to the U-boat, without having accomplished their mission. The fourth had disappeared in the darkness. Sometime later a distress signal was fired from the Very pistol but this only attracted the attention of the planes, which again attacked the U-boat.

On the morning of 7 August, the attack on *U-615* was resumed. At 0952Z in approximate position 12° 27′ N, 64° 54′ W, she flooded and sank. The survivors were in the water slightly over an hour when they were rescued by USS *Walker*. *Walker* picked up three officers, 40 men, and the dead body of the wounded petty officer. The prisoners were put ashore at Trinidad.

CHAPTER FIFTEEN

Voyage Not Completed

It could be said that Blue Star's *Melbourne Star* had seen more than her fair share of the dark side of the war. Bombed by a Focke-Wulf while off the west coast of Ireland in the opening stages of the war, she had twice run the gauntlet to Malta, firstly with Operation SUBSTANCE in July 1941, and again with Operation PEDESTAL a year later. On each occasion she had been sorely tested, but never found wanting. Released from Admiralty service after PEDESTAL, she slipped back into her old role, carrying general cargo outward from British ports, returning with frozen lamb and wool from Australia and New Zealand. She was back earning her keep again and the war was just another side issue, annoying and dangerous perhaps, but unavoidable.

While the *Melbourne Star* was thus engaged the war moved on apace; the Japanese bombed Pearl Harbor, and the Far East was in flames, with British forces heavily involved. In consequence, when she sailed from Liverpool on 22 March 1943, instead of the usual innocuous mixture of manufactured goods she carried in her holds 8,285 tons of shells, bombs and torpedoes, topped off with crated aircraft on deck. It was Malta all over again.

Captain David MacFarlane, awarded the OBE for his work in the Malta convoys, had also moved on, and in command of the *Melbourne Star* was 57-year-old Captain James Bennett-Hall, a seasoned veteran who had survived the sinking of an earlier command, the passenger liner *Andalucia Star* in October 1942. Bennett-Hall had with him a crew of seventy-six, many of whom had been with the ship in Operation PEDESTAL, eleven DEMS gunners, and thirty-one passengers, including twelve women and two children.

After clearing the River Mersey, the *Melbourne Star* sailed north overnight to anchor off Greenock, in the Firth of Clyde, to await a westbound Atlantic convoy to New York. With a less vulnerable cargo, the 17-knot vessel would have crossed the Atlantic alone, but in view of increased U-boat activity in the Western

Approaches it was considered wise that she should be in convoy, at least until clear of the worst of the danger.

Convoy ON 175, consisting of 40 merchant ships, most of them in ballast, left the shelter of the Clyde early on 24 March. Its escort force, which joined in the North Channel later in the day, was massive, and determined to keep the U-boats at bay. On the morning of the 27th, when in longitude 25° West, and it was considered safe to do so, the *Melbourne Star* pulled out of the convoy, signalled her good-byes, and set a south-westerly course for the Caribbean and the Panama Canal.

As she pulled away from the other ships it was obvious that the weather was deteriorating, with a long heavy swell from the west being a sure indicator of something nasty brewing over the horizon. In spite of this Bennett-Hall, thoroughly fed up with conforming to the 'convoy plod', took great pleasure in ringing for full speed. The *Melbourne Star* surged forward, quickly leaving the convoy astern, and was soon riding the incoming swells at 17 knots. Within a couple of hours the ships of ON 175 were no more than a pall of smoke on the darkening horizon astern.

Apart from the worsening weather, the *Melbourne Star*'s transatlantic crossing proved to be uneventful, the only excitement being the sighting of a ship's lifeboat. A closer inspection showed the boat to be empty and abandoned, but it served as a grim reminder of the dangers that might lie ahead. Few other ships were sighted during the course of the passage, one that passed quite close being the Portuguese cargo/passenger liner *Amarante*, later said to be a German commerce raider in disguise. However, she made no attempt to interfere with the *Melbourne Star*.

Due to the highly volatile nature of his cargo, as they neared the Caribbean Captain Bennett-Hall began to steer a zig-zag course during daylight hours and posted extra lookouts around the clock. However, despite the extra eyes watching the horizon, no one saw the periscope which had been following discreetly in the *Melbourne Star*'s wake throughout the daylight hours of 1 April.

U-129, a Type IXC boat sailing under the command of *Korvettenkapitän* Hans-Ludwig Witt had left her base at Lorient three weeks earlier, and was also bound for the Caribbean Sea, having come upon the British ship by chance. Witt had achieved phenomenal success in the area during the course of Operation DRUMBEAT in early 1942, and was back to try his luck again.

Operation DRUMBEAT had been mounted to coincide with the Japanese attack on Pearl Harbor in December 1941, six long-range Type IXCs having crossed the Atlantic with the intention of hitting the Americans while they were otherwise occupied. Even though the US had then been at war with Germany for some months, no coastwise convoys had yet been organized for merchant ships, which were still sailing unprotected, as they had been in time of peace. Ships were unarmed, unescorted, and showing undimmed navigation lights at night. Furthermore, no attempt had been made to dim the lights ashore. Coastal towns were still brilliantly lit and lighthouses, beacons and buoys were still on full power.

One ship a day was being lost in mysterious circumstances off America's east coast, and this was being put down to undiscovered mines laid by the odd German submarine. As for the US Navy, the few ships not occupied with the Japanese in the Pacific were acting as though the war was on another planet. Meanwhile, Dönitz's Type IXCs were laying about them with gay abandon, sinking almost unopposed more than 2 million tons of US and Allied shipping. During this American 'Happy Time', Hans-Ludwig Witt and *U-129* alone had accounted for 94,834 tons. Now they were back for more.

U-129's lookouts had first sighted the *Melbourne Star* when she was hull-down on the horizon about an hour before sunset on 1 April, and Witt had remained on the surface until her identity was clear. At 12,806 tons gross she was unusually large for a merchantman of her day, and as she was also fast, Witt approached cautiously, half-suspecting she might be an armed merchant cruiser. It was not until *U-129* was within 10 miles of her potential target that Witt was satisfied that the *Melbourne Star* was no more than a fast British cargo liner sailing alone. He then submerged to periscope depth and waited for darkness.

The sun set at 1800 hrs on the dot, as is the norm in tropical latitudes, and within half an hour it was completely dark. *U-129* then resurfaced and began to manoeuvre into position for the kill. It was a fine, clear night with a bright moon, but it was blowing a full gale from the west with a very rough sea. It was past midnight before Witt was able to get withing striking distance.

Second Officer Bill Richards, a 31-year-old Welshman from the Vale of Glamorgan, was keeping the middle watch on the bridge of the *Melbourne Star*. At the best of times the midnight to 4 am watch, with its interrupted sleep pattern, is not an easy watch to keep, and that night was no exception. Richards was tired and bored, longing for his bunk. At about 0300, an hour when life is said to be at its lowest ebb, he swept the horizon with his binoculars, found it as empty as before, and retired to the chart room to write up the log.

Able Seaman Len White was off watch and sound asleep in the crew's quarters aft when, at 0323 hrs, two torpedoes slammed into the hull of the *Melbourne Star*, striking just abaft the bridge house and laying her boiler room open to the sea. A third torpedo followed seconds later, going home forward of the bridge in No.2 hold, which was packed with high explosives. The resultant explosion was catastrophic, literally blowing the ship apart.

For 21-year-old Len White, thrown from his bunk and scrabbling for his life jacket in the dark, it was his worst nightmare all over again. Some ten months earlier he had been serving in the steamer *Norman Prince* in the West Indies when she had been torpedoed in similar circumstances. A short-sea trader of 1,913 tons gross, with a top speed of 8½ knots, the *Norman Prince*, through the necessities of war, was a long way from her usual Mediterranean waters. She was also sailing unescorted and, unknown to anyone on board, was being shadowed by Werner Hartenstein in *U-156*.

Hartenstein fired his first torpedo just after midnight, scoring a direct hit on the *Norman Prince*'s engine room, wrecking her main engine, blowing her starboard lifeboat overboard and covering the port, and only remaining, boat with smoking debris. As the sea cascaded into her broken hull the ship came slowly to a halt and began to settle quickly by the stern. Her crew, most of whom had been fast asleep when the torpedo struck, made a rush for the port boat. In the ensuing confusion only Third Officer Harry Jennings and ten others managed to board this boat before it was swept away by the swell. The rest of the survivors resorted to the liferafts, but as they were launching them Hartenstein delivered the *coup de grâce* with another single torpedo which hit between Nos 2 and 3 holds. This was just too much for the little ship. Her hull blasted open along much of its length, the *Norman Prince* went down with a rush, taking sixteen of her crew with her. Others were left struggling in the water until Jennings came to their rescue. For the next twenty-four hours the grossly overcrowded lifeboat was tossed about at the mercy of the wind and waves, being finally rescued by the Vichy French steamer *Angoulême*. The survivors were interned in Martinique until they were repatriated, four months later.

Leonard White's experience when the *Melbourne Star* blew up was no less harrowing, ending in his joining a handful of survivors struggling in the turbulent sea, with little apparent hope of rescue. He was one of eleven men who managed to scramble aboard three Carley floats which had floated clear when the ship went down. They were all who were left alive of the *Melbourne Star*'s total complement of 119 – seven men on one float, four on another and one on the third. The floats stayed together for a while then, buffeted by the waves, drifted apart and were lost to each other in the night. Two were never seen again, leaving Able Seaman Leonard White, Greaser William Best, Greaser William Burns, and 18-year-old Ordinary Seaman Ronald Nunn huddled miserably together on the remaining Carley float. They had food, they had water, but no protection from the elements. In July 1943, Scottish-born William Best was interviewed by the *Liverpool Echo*:

> He, William Best, was also sound asleep when the torpedo hit the ship. It received a second torpedo and the ship tilted at such an angle that he was 'able to walk off' into the sea. He swam through the debris to a raft which he was lucky to find in the inky darkness. When daylight came he saw another raft close by with three men on it. They pulled towards each other and it was decided to use his raft for the four of them. There was another raft apparently with seven men on it in the distance. They never saw this raft again after the first day. Their only protection on the raft against the blazing heat of the day and the biting cold at night, with often blustery rain squalls, was a tent rigged up from a sail.
>
> 'We had three meals a day of one biscuit, one piece of milk chocolate, two meat extract tablets and 2 ounces of water from a 20 gallon cask. Our diet began to affect us, and then we had some luck. Len White, an AB from the Birmingham District, caught a small fish with his hands.

He was soon making a fish hook from a tin opener and a
line from a piece of rope he untwisted. The first two days
we caught all kinds of fish and there was one fish about a
foot or so long and dark looking, which when opened up
melted in the mouth.'

Witt brought *U-129* to the surface as soon as it was light and
motored through the wreckage of the *Melbourne Star* looking for
clues to the identity of his victim. Having drawn a blank there,
he approached the only Carley float in sight, intent on questioning the few survivors on board. Able Seaman Len White,
who in the absence of an officer had assumed command of the
float, answered Witt's questions as far as giving the name of his
ship, but was careful not to mention the true nature of her cargo.
'Bound Panama with general supplies' was all he was prepared
to reveal. Anxious to leave the scene of his conquest quickly, Witt
accepted this, and *U-129* was soon stern-on and motoring away at
full speed. No assistance had been offered to the survivors.

   Alone on a hostile ocean, the four men on the Carley float took
stock of their situation. The lockers of the float contained eight
tins of biscuits, a few tins of malted milk tablets, chocolate in
tins, tins of pemmican meat extract and 22 gallons of drinking
water. There was also a tin of massage oil, intended to combat
frostbite. It was not much, but amongst four it could well mean
the difference between survival and death. And as a boost to the
already rising morale on board, the sun had come out, the wind
had dropped and the sea was calming.

   The four men were adrift on the Carley float for thirty-eight
days, during which time Leonard White's improvised fishing
line supplemented their meagre rations by a regular catch of one
or two edible fish each day. It was not much, but it helped to
make life almost bearable. There was nothing, however to pro-
tect them from the elements; they suffered the heat of the sun
beating down on them during the day and endured bitter cold
at night, when the temperature fell to just a few degrees above
freezing. Each morning as it grew light they eagerly searched the
horizon for the sign of a ship, but as day followed day there was
nothing, not even a wisp of smoke to bring encouragement. It
was as though they were existing in a small, isolated world of
their own. The excruciating boredom, the apparent hopelessness

of their situation gradually took their toll, until they were ready to just lie down and die. Then, in the afternoon of Sunday, 9 May, their thirty-ninth day adrift, came rescue. William Best told the *Liverpool Echo*:

> On the 39th day Ronald Nunn yelled that he was sure there was a plane above and then a flying boat began to circle overhead, obviously having seen us, and landed on the sea close by. An American lieutenant came to us in the plane's rubber dinghy and when he said 'Where are you guys from?' we just told him we were British. We offered him the fish that we'd caught that day. They were our most prized possession. They made us most comfortable on the flying boat and whipped us away to the Bermudas where they put us immediately into hospital. We were flying a couple of hours or more and ambulances were all ready for us when the plane landed.

The aircraft that picked up the four survivors was a Catalina flying boat of the US Navy, piloted by Lieutenant M. Kauffman. She was then on an anti-submarine patrol 250 miles out from Bermuda. When examined by doctors at the US Naval Hospital, despite having spent nearly six weeks on the Carley float, apart from suffering the usual effects from such long exposure to the wind and weather, the British seamen were found to be remarkably well. After three weeks in the hospital, they were discharged and repatriated to the United Kingdom.

On 15 August 1944, William Best, William Burns, Ronald Nunn and Leonard White were each awarded the British Empire Medal, the citation for which read:

> Able Seaman White, Greaser Burns, Greaser Best and Ordinary Seaman Nunn all displayed outstanding qualities of courage, fortitude and endurance which enabled them to survive the hardship and perils of the long and hazardous ordeal on the raft.

Blue Star Line were obviously less pleased. On arriving home, the survivors found that the company had stopped their wages the moment they went over the rail of the *Melbourne Star* into the water, and that those long and perilous days and nights spent on the unprotected Carley float were be counted as 'survivors' leave'.

Meanwhile, they were off pay until a berth in another ship was found for them, or they chose to go elsewhere. It may be that Blue Star were adhering strictly to maritime law as it was then written, but few other British shipping companies would have applied that law so harshly, certainly not in the case of men who had been through such an ordeal.

Leonard White and William Best continued at sea in British ships, and survived the war. Little is known of the subsequent movements of William Burns, while the other 'hero of the British Empire', 18-year-old Ronald Nunn, having had his fill of deep waters, went into the coastal trade believing he would be safer closer to home. He was to be proved wrong.

A little more than a year after Nunn and his three fellow survivors were plucked from the Atlantic by the American Catalina, the tide had turned in favour of the Allies and Germany was facing retribution. On the morning of 6 June 1944, a huge armada of 6,939 ships carrrying 156,115 Allied troops and their equipment crossed the English Channel to the invasion beaches of Normandy. They were led by 200 minesweepers who cleared eight swept channels through the German minefields, while bringing up the rear were some 300 British coasters loaded with ammunition and fuel to sustain the initial assault. In the ranks of this ragged assembly of John Masefield's 'dirty British coasters' was the 621-ton *Dunrange,* in which was serving Ordinary Seaman Ronald Nunn.

Owned by the Dunrange Steamship Company of Grangemouth, and commanded by Captain John Herbert, the *Dunrange* had been built in 1914, and despite being involved in two devastating world wars, was still plying her trade around the British coast, seemingly immune to the bombs, shells and torpedoes of the enemy. When the time came for Allied forces to return to the Continent, her potential was recognized by the Admiralty and she was requisitioned as a supply ship for Operation OVERLORD.

Also requisitioned by the Admiralty, and forming the core of the assault force, were 864 British and American deep-sea merchantmen, a number of them seasoned gauntlet runners. Prominent amongst them was a veteran of the Malta convoys, the 7,526-ton cargo liner *Clan Lamont,* commanded by the fiery Captain Angus Campbell, OBE. The *Clan Lamont* was carrying men of the 3rd Canadian Infantry Division, who were to be put ashore on Juno Beach using the ten infantry landing craft slung from davits on the ship's foredeck. True to form, Campbell was defying authority by flying the Scottish lion rampant in place of the Red Ensign, and carried his own piper, who would play the ship into action when the time came. It was a magnificent piece of theatre designed to boost morale, something which Angus Campbell was well known for.

The initial assault, as anticipated, was met by fierce German resistance. It is estimated that the German fortification, the Atlantic Wall as it was known, was manned by 80,000 troops under the command of General Erwin Rommel, hero of the North African campaign, most of whom were from the Eastern Front resting in what was thought to be a 'quiet area'. Inevitably, the casualties on both side were very heavy. Lance Corporal Reginald Clarke, who was with an advance party of the Royal Engineers aboard the *Clan Lamont*, gave a graphic description of the landing:

6th June 1944. 0930hours.

Our landing craft was now speeding through the black cloud of acrid smoke. Plumes of waterspouts were shooting up left, right and centre as the mortars and shells came down. I felt a sharp veer to the right, probably to avoid an underwater obstacle and for the first time we heard the bark of small arms overhead as we came into shore very fast. The OC and I had now positioned ourselves to observe the beach coming into view to identify the coloured beach marker flag. . . . It was very difficult to see anything for all the sea spray and smoke. There was a terrific jarring, grating sound underneath, as though the whole bottom of the craft was being torn out. We all lurched forward with the impact. I gripped my rifle hard. The stench of spilled diesel oil and cordite stung my nose and made my eyes water. Two explosions occurred just about fifty yards to our left and water spurted up and showered down onto our craft in an absolute deluge. The assault craft surged back a bit from the beach, then moved forward again, dug in and held, 'bottomed'. Crash! Down went the armour plated front and we had our first, but very brief, view of the beach. The O.C. yelled 'Clarke, look for the marker flag what's its colour?' It was green!

We had landed on MIKE GREEN, right off our target, we were supposed to be on NAN RED. I ran up the beach and dived for cover behind a sand dune, to my right were some of the first wave troops in the same location. I saw the Cpl. I had befriended laying in the prone position as if to fire his weapon, called to him but there was no response, he was dead.

An assault craft, broadside onto the beach, lay on its side next to us. It was shattered; not a single Canadian soldier or the crew had made it. It was a bloody mess, two bodies were actually hanging from the side, where they had been blown by the force of the explosion. The clothing on the lower parts of their bodies, which were badly mutilated, [was] missing and large streaks of red ran down the side of the assault craft to the sea where their life blood had drained away.

Obstacles were everywhere; one vicious looking pronged object with heavy explosive devices hung around the prongs was to our right. Quite a number of damaged assault craft, some on fire, were beached. There were armoured assault vehicles damaged and shattered by gunfire were lying inert, not clear of the water as the tide was still coming in.

At the uppermost part of the beach I saw firing coming from a bombed house, just beyond the formidable sea wall of concrete. A nasty wire fence just in front of the concrete wall was decorated with the sprawled bodies of about twenty Canadians; one was headless, God only knows what had hit him. But the most ironic was one young infantryman being supported by the fence in a kneeling and praying position!

The only thing in my mind now was to GO! and get to the beach. I was so tense, like a coiled spring ready to move like mad when I was told. I felt a bit numb and scared, and not ashamed to admit it.

A Beachmaster Major was standing right out on the open beach at the water's edge bellowing his instructions to the incoming assault through a megaphone held to his mouth. He was a very brave man ignoring his dangerous surroundings.

Short, sharp blasts on infantry whistles. No time to think now. Out at the double into about four feet of water, just about up to my chest. I touched bottom and forced myself forward . . .

On the afternoon of 9 June, D-Day plus 3, the *Dunrange* was fully loaded with ammunition and fuel and anchored off the Solent with thirteen other coasters, similarly loaded, ready to embark on her third crossing to the Normandy beachheads. The ships were to sail in convoy, designated ETC 4W, but would be unescorted, and timed to arrive off the beaches at dawn on the 10th.

Although the Channel crossing was a mere 80 miles, only eight hours steaming in darkness for the coasters, it was not without risk. German E-boats were known to be operating in the area, and had already mounted several attacks on British supply convoys.

The E-boat, the German equivalent of the British motor torpedo boat, was a very formidable craft which had operated against Allied convoys in the North Sea with considerable success in the past. One hundred and fifteen feet long, the E-boat was powered by three Daimler-Benz marine diesels, giving it a top speed of 48 knots and a cruising range of 800 miles. It was armed with two 21-inch torpedo tubes and four torpedoes, a 37mm AA gun and three 20mm quick firers. With a maximum draught of only 4 feet 10 inches, the E-boat was ideally suited for operations in the shallow waters of the English Channel and North Sea. Boats of the 9th Flotilla, based in Cherbourg, had been the first to meet the Allied invasion fleet on the morning of 6 June, but faced with such a vast assembly of transports, escorted by an equally vast number of warships, including battleships, cruisers and destroyers, they were reduced to making a half-hearted attack, firing their torpedoes at maximum range before turning tail and racing for the safety of Cherbourg's breakwaters. All the torpedoes missed their targets.

Now, three days later, the 9th Flotilla had returned and was exacting its revenge on the unescorted ships of Convoy ETC 4W, every one of which was fully loaded with a lethal mix of high explosives and petrol.

The *Dunrange* was just 35 miles north of the Normandy beachheads when the night sky was ripped apart by a violent explosion as the ship ahead of her, the 657-ton *Brackenfield* was hit by a torpedo. One blinding flash, and she was gone, vaporized.

The immediate, and instinctive reaction of Captain John Herbert, on the bridge of the *Dunrange*, was to close the sticken ship to pick up survivors, but as he altered course towards the dying glow, two E-boats appeared out of the darkness, one on each bow. There was no escape. The 10-knot, single-screw coaster was standing straight into the jaws of death.

Two torpedoes streaked towards the *Dunrange*, one fired from either side. Neither was seen from the bridge of the coaster, but even if they had been spotted, it was too late for Captain Herbert to take avoiding action. One torpedo shot across the bows of the *Dunrange*, missing her by a few feet, but the other ran true, and its 940 lb high-explosive warhead, combined with the coaster's cargo of ammunition and petrol simply blew her apart. Only two of her crew survived the explosion. Ordinary Seaman Ronald Nunn was not one of them.

Conclusions

This book is by way of a fond farewell to an era fast disappearing into the mists of time; an era of long, lazy sea passages with Sparks at his key and 'He Who Must Be Obeyed' ensconced in his eyrie below the bridge, of sextants at the ready and the mournful wail of fog horns in the Channel.

It was the time of the cargo liners, once the elite of British shipping, but now all gone, swept away on a tide of high-rise cruise ships and monster container carriers. Men like Angus Campbell and David MacFarlane, the calculated risk takers of the liner trade, are no more. They have been replaced by a new breed of computer-compliant automatons, who, through the wonders of modern communications, dance to the tune of 'Head Office' twenty-four/seven.

The sheer joy of challenging the unknown has been sacrificed on the altar of 'Health & Safety' and 'wokeness'. No decision can be taken without a full risk assessment being made, no work, however urgent, may be carried out without a written permit from a head of department. Going to sea is no longer the great adventure eagerly sought after by the young. What was once a chosen calling is now just another job, as boring and predictable as driving a No. 11 bus.

Along the way, the Red Ensign, once famed for its integrity and expertise, has become another flag of convenience, under which foreign owners are free to register their ships, pay token service to the law, and employ multinational crews, while British seamen languish on the dole.

Britain would do well to remember that an island nation without its own ships is a nation in thrall to others. And if war should come again, who would rally to the sound of Drake's drum now that the Gauntlet Runners have gone?

No one can be singled out to be solely to blame for this sickening demise of British merchant shipping. It is something that has happened over the years, partly through apathy, partly through the emergence of nations which were once under the yoke of others. The latter was inevitable, the apathy is inexcusable.

Bibliography

Admiralty, *East of Malta, West of Suez*, HMSO, 1943
Course, Captain A. G., *Deep Sea Tramp*, Hollis & Carter, 1960
Devine, A. D., *Dunkirk*, Faber & Faber, 1945
Elliot, Peter, *The Cross and the Ensign*, Granada, 1982
Falls, Cyril, *The Second World War*, Methuen, 1948
Hoyt, Edwin P., *U-Boats*, McGraw-Hill Book Company, 1987
Hunter, Shackland, *Malta Convoy*, Fontana, 1963
Laskier, Frank, *My Name is Frank*, Allen & Unwin, 1941
Mallmann Showell, J. P., *U-Boats Under the Swastika*, Ian Allan, 1973
Montgomery, Michael, *Who Sank the Sydney?*, Leo Cooper, 1981
Muggenthaler, August Karl, *German Raiders of World War II*,
    Macmillan, 1980
Robertson, Terence, *The Golden Horseshoe*, Evans Bros Ltd., 1955
Slader, John, *The Fourth Service*, Robert Hale, 1994
Slader, John, *The Red Duster at War*, William Kimber, 1988
Thomas, David A., *Malta Convoys*, Leo Cooper, 2003
Woodman, Richard, *The Real Cruel Sea*, John Murray, 2004

Other Sources

National Archives, Kew
National Maritime Museum
Imperial War Museum
BBC Archives
Sea Breezes magazine https://seabreezes.co.im/
Various internet websites

Index